VELVET ANTLER

Nature's Superior Tonic

Alison Davidson

New Century Publishers 2000
East Canaan, Connecticut

VELVET ANTLER
Nature's Superior Tonic

ISBN 0-9701110-0-2
Library of Congress Catalog Card Number # 00-132928

Printed in Canada
May 2000

Published by New Century Publishers 2000
Marketing Office USA
283 East Canaan Rd.
P.O. Box 36
East Canaan, CT 06024
(860) 824-5301

Marketing Office Canada
60 Bullock Dr. Unit 6
Markham, ON L3P3P2
(905)-471-7885

Acknowledgments

I would like to thank the following for their generous help in the research of this book: Thomas Brown, my partner and editor; Dr Helen Zhou, doctor of traditional Chinese medicine now living in New Zealand; M.J. Loza and Murdoch Dryden of the New Zealand Game Industry Board for access to invaluable research material; Dr Jimmy Suttie, AgResearch, Invermay, leader of the Velvet Antler Research Program in New Zealand; Shelley and Clint Thomsen of Gevir Products, Hawkes Bay; Cliff Bellaney of Glenalbany Nutriceuticals Limited, Christchurch; Harry Bimler of Tarawera Deerpark; Tim and Mary Hope of Tia Maha deer farm, Hawkes Bay; Mr Lim from a traditional herb shop in Chinatown, San Francisco, who initiated my journey into the mysteries of Chinese herbalism; Chris Ward, Chinese Herbalist, Mount Maunganui; Michael, Jane and James Davidson for many visits to their deer farm at Te Tohe Station, Hawkes Bay; my mother Carol and brother Stuart Davidson, always willing to experiment with exotic remedies; my daughter Tara and Mathew Hart Design, Auckland, for cover design, and many others who may not have known they were part of the research.

Contents

Left: fully formed hard antler. Right: velvet antler

INTRODUCTION

A mong the several thousand herbs used in Chinese traditional medicine, there is a small but elite group known since ancient times as the 'kingly' or 'Imperial' herbs. These were the tonic herbs used by emperors and sages, the wealthy and discerning; very special herbs that were recognized as having extraordinary health promoting benefits for those fortunate, or wealthy enough to acquire them.

While relatively unknown in the West, many of these wonderful tonic herbs have a history of continuous use dating back thousands of years, and they are still in use today for one reason only—*because they work.*

Among these kingly herbs, and ranking alongside ginseng as one of the most precious of all, is deer antler velvet, rapidly proving its reputation in the West as an outstanding energy tonic and adaptogen.

Although not technically regarded as a herb, but rather as a 'harmonizing remedy,' deer antler velvet has been prized for over two thousand years in the Orient for its unique tonic and stimulating effects. It is among the most highly valued and expensive remedies used throughout Asia and is regarded as the prime tonic for promoting endurance, stamina and strength. Its reputation as an aphrodisiac commonly held by Westerners may add to the mystique of velvet antler, but only touches upon the surface of its wide-ranging therapeutic properties.

Quite apart from its high nutritional content of minerals and amino acids, the growth factors so far identified in velvet are highly significant for natural anti-aging programmes and growth hormone therapy research.

As a renaissance of herbalism and natural medicine spreads throughout the West, much attention is being focused on remedies which can treat the whole person in a gentle and balanced way. As the claims of traditional practitioners are increasingly becoming validated by scientific research, a process of integration between alternative and allopathic medicine is taking place. What was regarded as alternative yesterday, may well be a part of mainstream medicine by tomorrow.

While velvet antler has been extensively researched and used clinically in Russia since the 1930's, recent interest in this complex substance has been aroused by the results of a unique scientific testing programme carried out in New Zealand. These results are capturing the attention of scientists in the West and exciting clinical researchers with the possible uses of velvet antler in the area of mainstream medicine.

To date, these groundbreaking tests have shown deer velvet antler:

- to stimulate the immune system, the body's main line of defence against infection and disease

- to contain anti-inflammatory agents which may assist in reducing the pain and inflammation of a variety of degenerative diseases

• to contain marked anabolic or growth stimulating properties, including the growth factors IGF-1 and IGF-2.

• to increase muscular strength and endurance

• to significantly reduce the damaging side effects of chemotherapy drugs, while at the same time increasing their effectiveness

It can be seen here that the potential applications of velvet antler in Western medicine and natural health care are enormous. It's only a matter of time, according to the Game Industry Board who closely monitors the farming of domestic deer in New Zealand, before "...velvet will become as accepted in Western countries as vitamins and other dietary supplements."

On the other side of the Pacific, scientists at the University of Alberta in Edmonton, Canada, are evaluating the role of velvet antler in nutriceuticals, functional and medical foods. In April 2000, they hosted the first Antler Science and Product Technology Symposium in Banff, where thirty papers were presented by leading velvet antler researchers from around the world.

The American natural health movement is already promoting velvet as one of the most promising new supplements for the millenium and beyond, including alternative health care pioneer Betty Kamen who states in her book *The Remarkable Healing Power of Velvet Antler*: "Taken together, ancient tradition and new research validating the benefits of velvet antler make a compelling case for its inclusion in every healthful diet."

Written to serve as an introduction to this ancient and powerful remedy, *Velvet Antler* briefly covers the history and tradition of velvet's use, the scientific research which supports these traditional claims, together with examples of velvet's well-documented therapeutic benefits. Hopefully it will answer some of the most commonly asked questions about velvet antler, which truly is, as the subtitle states, *nature's superior tonic.*

Velvet antler at its prime for medicinal use.
photo courtesy of Shelley & Clint Thomsen

I

BACKGROUND

*As smooth as velvet, as soft as fur are the stag's
young antlers. It's hard to imagine the knife-like
racks of bone growing silently within to break forth
like a tree already formed in perfect symmetry from
the soft earth, like a finely honed weapon drawn
from its velvet sheath.*

Velvet is the name given to deer antlers while they are growing and still in a cartilaginous state, and while bone is forming. In this state they have a soft velvet-like covering and in Scotland, ancestral home of many of the wild red deer found in New Zealand, this soft, furry velvet was known as 'moss' or 'down'.

Regarded with an almost supernatural reverence throughout the ancient world deer have fed, clothed and provided humanity with medicine since the earliest days of recorded history. From Scotland and Ireland to Sicily and Arcadia the stag, or man-stag bearing antlers is a powerful recurring figure, a royal symbol of the king, a symbol of power, virility and regeneration.

Across the Atlantic deer have also held a special place in native American life and myth providing antlers for tools, weapons, jewelry and powerful medicine. The deer was so highly regarded its image was seen as a constellation in the night sky. This great respect with which the deer was regarded extended to other cultures as well, from Europe and America to the shamanic customs of Russia and Lappland, and further east to the ancient medicinal traditions of Asia. Records exist in China describing the use of deer antler velvet as a medicine over two thousand years ago and it has continued to be one of the fundamental ingredients in traditional Oriental medicine down through the centuries until the present time.

There is a widespread belief, even today, that velvet antler possesses powerful aphrodisiac qualities and that is the reason why it is so keenly sought by Asian buyers. It is true that velvet has been used since ancient times for its tremendous energy producing qualities, and it is undoubtedly an ingredient of many elixirs and herbal formulas that are claimed to be aphrodisiac. This is not surprising considering the important role that antlers play in the sexual life of the deer. The larger the antlers the more potent the stag is considered to be and the largest, superior grade velvet is traditionally regarded as much more valuable than the smaller antlers.

But the true value of velvet lies in the extraordinarily wide range of its applications which was known and appreciated not only in the Orient, but also in Europe where it was once a common medicinal item in the traditional Galenic apothecary.[1] According to the ancient Roman Plinius Secundus, antlers contained "some sort of healing drug" and he described its use in the treatment of epilepsy.

Currently the major producers of velvet antler are New Zealand (the largest with an annual production of 450 tons), China, Korea, Russia, the United States and Canada. While deer farming has long been a traditional way of life in China, up until the middle of the 19th century velvet antler was obtained in Russia by hunting deer in the wild. During the 1840s the domestication of Caspian red deer was begun in Russia in the southern Altai and later spread to other parts of Siberia. During the Soviet years deer farms were organised to supply the growing demand for velvet from Asia, especially the antler from the sika, or spotted deer, but also from the maral and wapiti. *Pantui* (the Russian name for velvet antler) was considered to be "a valuable medical raw material with an unlimited demand both in the overseas and internal market."[2]

Around the same time that deer farming began in Russia, feral red deer were being liberated into New Zealand from the royal parks in England and the Highlands of Scotland. Although not native to New Zealand they thrived on the lush vegetation and temperate climate, growing larger and more fertile than their original ancestral stock. In fact they thrived so well they became a menace to farmers and to the indigenous forests in which they roamed. A government policy of extermination failed as the herds had become so well entrenched in the high rugged mountains, but over time the idea of farming deer took root. By the time it was sanctioned by law in 1969, a year after the first feral deer were captured from the high country and relocated to an experimental farm, a new era in New Zealand's history of farming was born.

With the growth of deer farming and an increasing demand for velvet antler from Asia, there came a curious marriage of interests. Korean doctors of traditional medicine invited to inspect the deer farms were impressed with the natural environment in which the deer were thriving, while New Zealand farmers through their contact with Asian traders were exposed to a very unconventional tradition of medicine—at least in Western terms.

The pioneers in this field stepped across into an ancient tradition and philosophy of health and found themselves at the forefront of scientific research into the efficacy of one of Oriental medicine's most valuable remedies. Due to this pioneering spirit and the high standards of quality maintained in the industry, New Zealand is now regarded as producing among the finest velvet antler in the world, and its unique scientific programme is at the forefront of world research into the medicinal properties of velvet.

Antlers naturally grow with extraordinary swiftness and are cast at the end of winter for the cycle to repeat itself the following year. They are harvested as velvet while still in a cartilaginous state, before they harden into bone, without harming the deer which are very valuable animals.

Over recent years deer farmers have spent millions of dollars perfecting the breed by importing animals either directly to New Zealand, or even by sending breeding animals to England and then importing their progeny. The genealogy of the finest stags and hinds are recounted with the pride and reverence once reserved for racehorses, and highly sophisticated techniques of artificial insemination and embryo transplants have tempered the primal instinct of the roar. Not only red deer but elk, wapiti, fallow, sika, rusa and sambar are among the deer bred today, magnificent animals rivaling the best of their species to be found anywhere in the world.

Also keen to explore the health benefits of the velvet they were supplying to Asia, companies born from the early days of deer farming have introduced their velvet antler products to the market at home and abroad. Today you can find capsuled velvet powder in health food stores and pharmacies, or velvet combined with traditional tonic herbs such as ginseng. Velvet extracts are a growing industry, either sold alone or in combination with a range of herbs, sometimes in alcohol as potent tonic elixirs and liqueurs. Velvet antler can also be purchased blended with honey, or combined into luxurious cosmetic creams and lotions. As the public becomes aware of its unique properties the prospects for new and original products incorporating this ancient remedy are truly exciting.

NOTES

1. Holmes, Peter, *Jade Remedies: A Chinese Herbal Reference for the West,* Snow Lotus Press, Boulder (1997)
2. Archer, Dr. R.H., and Palfreyman, P. J., *Properties of New Zealand Deer Velvet, Part I, Search of the Literature, Vol. 1,* for Massey University and Wrightson NMA Ltd. (1983)

2

VELVET ANTLER IN ORIENTAL MEDICINE

English	*Velvet Antler*
Mandarin	*Lu Rong*
Cantonese	*Lok Yan*
Korean	*Nogyong*
Japanese	*Rokujo*

For millennia velvet antler has been prized throughout Asia for its wide-ranging medicinal and health promoting qualities. Among the many thousands of herbs used in traditional Oriental medicine velvet antler is one of the most important, in fact, one of the primary ingredients used in this ancient tradition. It is still consumed today by millions of people in Asia who regard it as a major tonic for promoting strength and stamina, for maintaining good health and preventing illness.

There are few natural remedies known in the world that are held to be as precious as velvet antler, and in order to understand its role in traditional medicine it may be helpful to take a brief overview of Oriental health philosophy.

Fundamental to its practice is the concept of *yin* and *yang*—the cosmic forces which are said to control all natural phenomena and life processes. In every cyclic process in nature, in the cosmos as well as in the human body these two energetic principles can be observed at work, as for example, in day and night, summer and winter, life and death. They are like energy moving between the two poles of a battery—the yang which is expansive and active and the yin which is inward and concentrated.

In the human body, yin is said to govern the blood and yang controls the *ch'i*, the life force, or vital energy. While blood carries the essential nutrients through the body to produce the ch'i, ch'i is the force which carries blood throughout the body. So it can be seen that both of these forces are mutually dependent and the ideal state of health, both within the body and within the universe, is reached when these two forces are in balance and harmony.

Traditional Oriental medicine seeks to maintain or restore this balance within the individual, emphasising the prevention of illness which is said to result when this state of harmony is disrupted.

> When a disease appears in one part of the body, Oriental medicine does not limit its treatment to that part alone but treats the entire body and works to achieve an ideal physiological and spiritual balance, thereby bringing about a complete cure and a return to a state of total health.[1]

It is the doctor's duty to maintain the good health and vitality of his clients—in marked contrast to Western medicine which generally focuses on treating the symptoms of disease, although it is now recognized that the demand for complementary and alternative medicine is rapidly growing in the West. A recent survey showed that one out of every three Americans had tried some form of alternative health therapy.

Deeply interwoven with this wholistic philosophy of health maintenance is the preparation and use of herbal tonics, among these being velvet antler, said to be the most powerful of all animal-derived medicines and one of the most valuable. At the Research Institute in Harbin, Northern China, it is regarded as "the second most important ingredient in Oriental medicine after ginseng."

Rather than being regarded purely as a medicinal, velvet is considered to be a tonic, or restorative, used to strengthen the life-force or *ch'i*, and to promote the body's adaptability to stress of all kinds. Above all, it is taken to build the perfect balance and harmony between body and mind which is behind the Oriental concept of 'radiant health'. Although there are thousands of herbs in the Chinese pharmacopeia which treat specific diseases, velvet is one of the select few that are regarded as pure tonics, and its history of use is impressive.

The first recorded use of deer velvet as a medicine in ancient times dates back over two thousand years to a Han tomb in Hunan Province in China where a silk scroll was recovered listing over fifty different diseases for which velvet antler was prescribed. Lao Shao, the god of longevity who smiles benignly down through the centuries and whose image is found in Chinese herbal literature and pharmacies around the world, is often shown holding tonic herbs in his hand while accompanied by a small spotted deer from which the antler was used, the native Chinese sika.

He was undoubtedly smiling on the master herbalist Li Shi Zhen, author of the 16th century medical classic *Pen Ts'ao Kang Mu,* which is perhaps the best record of the historical claims for velvet's therapeutic value. Li Shi Zhen spent his lifetime gathering and classifying all the available information on Chinese herbs, and this highly authoritative *materia medica* is the standard text of Chinese herbalists to this day. In its pages he describes over 1800 different substances traditionally used as medicinals, devoting several pages to deer products including velvet antler which was prepared into powders, pills, extracts, tinctures and ointments.

> Breckman (N.D.) lists Li Shih Chen's claims as the following: pantui (velvet antlers) increase the vital force, boost the will, strengthen the muscles and bones, cure general debility, impaired vision and hearing; they can be used for treating rheumatism, osteomyelitis, uterine haemorrhage, spermatorrhea and many other diseases. Continuous use of pantui delays the onset of senility.[2]

The exotically named 'spotted dragon pills', for instance, which include velvet antler together with herbal and other ingredients are recommended as a universal tonic, and a velvet herbal preparation extracted in wine, is recommended for treating 'sexual weakness'. A popular song from this classic poetically extols the virtues of velvet antler from the Chinese spotted deer for restoring the energy of one who has exhausted their sexual energy:

> *If you never curbed the passions,*
> *And squandered the ocean,*
> *The magic potion of nine metamorphoses,*
> *By concentrating slowly, will offer you heaven...*
> *The spotted dragon,*
> *A pearl on his brow,*
> *Will restore the lower cave—*
> *The portals of the jasper palace.*

Although widely reputed to be an aphrodisiac, and customarily used by Chinese men down through the centuries to increase their sexual potency, this is only one aspect of the wide ranging health benefits associated with the use of velvet antler. To put this in perspective, for example, in Korea women wishing to maintain their family's health are the largest buyers of velvet—which is a considerable amount as over eighty percent of the velvet produced in the world is currently consumed by Koreans.

In Korea the deer is very highly esteemed and regarded as a lucky animal with the greatest *yang*. Considered to be both "a tradition and a medicine" velvet antler is given predominantly to children in tonic preparations to promote growth and strong healthy bodies. Associated with health and longevity in a medical tradition that reaches back for thousands of years it is a vital ingredient in a great number of herbal formulas, with the proportion of velvet prescribed reflecting the prosperity of the client, and it is not a cheap medicine by any means, selling for between $US750 and $US1500 a kilo.

According to Dr Peter Yoon, a renowned and highly respected doctor of Oriental medicine in Korea, the first record of velvet's use was published in a Korean text *Shin Nong Bon Cho Kyun* over 1800 years ago. Referring to the deer as the symbol of long life and vitality, a translation of this text reads:

> There were many deer on South Hill and one male deer covers hundreds of female deer and its length of life is almost a thousand years and when the male deer reaches five hundred years old, the color of its skin becomes white.[3]

Along with this obvious reference to its power to increase virility, many health problems and their treatment with velvet (or *nogyong*) are described:

> Deer velvet tastes sweet and its property is warm. It is used for reinforcing vital energy, strengthening memory and will, generating teeth, curing persistent vaginal blood discharges, lochia (discharge following birth) and treating fevers and epilepsy.

It goes on to state:

> Deer antler cures sores, carbuncles (boils), expels pathogens as well as retained blood in the uterus. It is also used for treating consumptive disease and illness caused by overexertion, lumbago, excessive loss of

weight, repairing the body, reinforcing vital energy, curing infertility, stopping pain and preventing miscarriage. Prolonged consumption would keep the body light and extend longevity.

Almost two millennia later velvet antler is still one of the most highly regarded medicinals in Korea and thousands of pharmacists and doctors prescribe it daily, in combination with other herbs and brewed in the traditional way as a tea or soup.

NOTES

1. *Deer Antler Velvet: The medicine with 2000 years of history,* The Deer Farmer/New Zealand Game Industry Board (1992)
2. Archer, Dr. R. H., and Palfreyman, P. J., *Properties of New Zealand Deer Velvet, Part I, Search of the Literature, Vol. 1,* for Massey University and Wrightson NMA Ltd. (1983)
3. See note 1.

Sika stags in hard antler.
Photo courtesy Harry Bimler

Processed velvet slices of varying grades.

3

Traditional Uses

Just as ginseng is the most precious and effective of the plant harmony remedies, so these antlers, named 'pantui', are the choice animal harmony remedy.[1]

Traditionally regarded as a powerful rejuve-nating tonic, the more specific therapeutic claims made for velvet antler in Oriental medicine are extraordinarily extensive and wide-ranging. Velvet is still being prescribed today throughout Asia, as it has been over countless centuries for the following:

- promoting growth in children
- improving delayed development of teeth, closure of fontanelle
- development of skeletal system
- improving movement disorders such

as delayed walking in infants

- increasing blood in the body
- cardiovascular disorders (anaemia, low blood pressure or hypotomia)
- recovery from respiratory infection
- strengthening stamina
- improving mental development
- improving liver function
- treatment of diabetes mellitus
- strengthening immunity — prevention of disease
- treatment of atherosclerosis
- treating menstrual disorders and menopause in women
- endocrinological disorders, especially hypothyroidism
- gastrointestinal disorders (poor digestion, constipation)
- preventing aging and loss of memory
- promoting the reproductive function, infertility
- sexual disorders in men (impotence, watery semen, premature ejaculation hypertrophy of prostate gland)
- treatment of skin ulcers, skin complaints and psoriasis
- recuperation and regeneration of damaged tissue
- neurosis and facilitation of recovery from diseased state
- for treatment for cold extremities, lumbago, clear and profuse urine, weight loss, weak bones and sinews, cold hands and feet, dysmennorhoea and leukorrhoea[2,3]

This is an amazing list of human ailments to be covered by one simple remedy—it's no wonder velvet antler was regarded in dynastic times as the "Emperor's tonic". Because these claims are so extensive and cover such a wide range of symptoms, it may be helpful to simplify velvet's health benefits under the broad categories of restorative, nutritive and rejuvenative.[4]

This means that velvet is regarded in traditional medicine more as a powerful restorer and maintainer of health rather than as a cure for disease. Its function is seen to strengthen and protect the body rather than being an agent to fight pathogens and infection. It builds the body by building the blood and is regarded as a highly nutritious food, quite apart from its unique medicinal properties.

In the *Divine Husbandman's Classic of the Materia Medica*, velvet antler is classified as having sweet, salty and warm properties and is connected with the function of the Liver and Kidneys. Here it is said that velvet "tonifies the kidneys and fortifies the Yang", and is prescribed for impotence, premature ejaculation, coldness and weakness in the lower back.

It "tonifies and nourishes Qi [ch'i] and Blood," and strengthens the bones and sinews. It is used to treat children suffering from physical and/or mental development disorders, or skeletal deformities.

It should be noted here that when Chinese medicine refers to a herb or remedy being associated with the Kidneys and Liver, it is not only referring to the physical organs of the kidneys and liver but also to very specific energy flows through the body which involve these organs—a system of channels or pathways through which the vital force or ch'i circulates from one organ to another. These pathways are known as 'meridians' and are the basis of the traditional healing art of acupuncture.

There are twelve of these meridians and in order for all of the organs to be healthy, the ch'i energy must be flowing freely through each of the meridians. If the energy becomes blocked or the flow is insufficient problems arise in that part of the body, the organs cease functioning properly and illness can result. And this is where herbs play such an important role, as they are said to affect or to have an affinity with specific organ meridians.

Deer antler velvet in the Chinese *materia medica* is most strongly associated with the Kidney meridian, which includes the kidneys themselves as well as the adrenal glands. These very important glands produce a wide range of hormones with complex activities which include regulating the body's response to stress, regulating sugar metabolism, and directly controlling the reproductive hormone production of the gonads.

Of all the meridians the Kidney, known as the 'Root of Life,' is considered the most important, "since strong Kidney function provides power to all the other organic systems and serves as a reservoir of highly refined stored energy. For this reason, the Kidney tonics of Chinese tonic herbalism are among the most important."[5]

In their wisdom the ancient herbalists used velvet antler for conditions of deficient Kidney yang energy with the symptoms as mentioned previously, including exhaustion and weakness, lumbar pain, a depressed immune system, frequent infections, coldness, incontinence, impotence and infertility.

They knew that this most powerful of all animal remedies increased the natural flow of ch'i through the Kidney, thus helping to regulate the function of the adrenal cortex and restore the natural vitality of the individual.

> The aim is to restore the energy to its natural balance and flow... As the energy balances are corrected, the person's body, mind and spirit starts to heal.[6]

With its warming tonic properties velvet antler is traditionally taken before and during the winter months to strengthen the immune system and increase the body's resistance to stress and illness. It is an exceptional remedy for the elderly and is used as a general tonic for "debility, old age, impaired vision and hearing, rheumatism, uterine haemorrhage, spermatorrhoea, and other diseases."

As well as strengthening the immune functions one of its most important properties is to increase the production and circulation of blood in the body. For centuries deer velvet has been used "to control blood pressure, increase hemoglobin levels, increase lung efficiency, improve recuperation from exertion, improve muscle tone and glandular functions, sharpen mental alertness, relieve the inflammation of arthritis, and heal stomach ulcers."[7]

It is highly regarded for treating hormonal and sexual problems, which are included among many of the documented traditional uses for velvet, as the following reports indicate:

Wong and Wu (1936) reported velvet antler of sika deer ... prescribed for such maladies as vaginal bleeding, leucorrhea, convulsions of feverish colds, nymphomania, spermatorrhea, haematuria, enuresis, arthritis, backache, deafness, dimness of vision and vertigo. Velvet is said to benefit the vitality and strengthen the mind ... has a high curative value, raising the tone and vigour of the organism, improving heart action, eliminating fatigue and weakness of the heart muscle, and hastening the healing of abrasions, especially when they have become infected.[8]

Luick (1981) ... has listed divers [sic] claims made for velvet antler which include its effectiveness in cases of epilepsy, snake bite, anaemia, gout, deafness, rheumatism, ulcers, headaches, relief of hypertension, alleviation of the convulsions that attend cold exposure, improvement in the rate of wound healing, prevention of vaginal haemorrhage and spermatorrhea, dissolving of bladder stones and the treatment of nervous disorders associated with overwork, infection and menopause. In addition, velvet is said to be taken by women during the last trimester of pregnancy and during lactation.[9]

According to Dr Kong (1980) of the Chinese University of Hong Kong, the ethnomedical uses of velvet include treatment for anaemia, vertigo, frequent urination (all signs of debility), vaginal discharges, and other forms of female reproductive debility ... Velvet preparations increase muscle tone, increase lung efficiency and increase appetite. It acts like a male sex hormone, animal tests showing it to be about half the strength of testosterone. It is also good for wound healing.[10]

There are reports of velvet antler being used as a medicinal remedy in Russia during the 15th century where it was called "Horns of Gold," attesting to the high value placed on it. Russian healers of the mid 17th century recommended reindeer antlers for "epilepsy, headaches, and anaemia, and the fat from them for curing ulcers and rheumatism". Other researchers reported that the Russian natives often ate the tips of the growing reindeer antlers after roasting them over a fire.[11]

Today, according to Dr Yoon, deer velvet is prescribed by Korean physicians for anaemia, diabetes, to strengthen liver and kidney functions, to strengthen the immune system, for endocrine problems, improving the memory, arteriosclerosis and stress related problems. It is also clinically prescribed for sterility, prostation, dizziness and blood discharge. But most importantly, it is used as a tonic to promote growth, appetite and as a restorative. It is held to restore energy, to nourish the blood and improve mental power.

In Korea, it is a remedy for everyone in the family from babies, often taken to the doctor soon after their first birthday for their first prescription of velvet, to the elderly where it helps to strengthen their resistance to stress and stave off the chills of winter. Men take it for sexual disorders such as impotence, premature ejaculation and watery semen. Women are prescribed it for infertility, menstrual and menopausal problems. "Also," says Dr Yoon, "when a pregnant woman takes velvet powder during childbirth (one dose, four grams of velvet powder), it is very helpful for an easy delivery."[12]

He also describes the practise of 'aqua-acupuncture' which is used in Oriental medicine. In this practise, the deer velvet extract is injected into the appropriate meridian point on the human body and is especially effective for "sciatic neuritis, impotence, shoulder pain, neck stiffness and the after effects of paralysis."

In China, velvet antler is combined with herbs in mixtures and patent medicines, or processed into pills in modern pharmaceutical factories. At Chinese markets and herb shops a large variety of these pills are available, often blended with ginseng and other tonic herbs to enhance their effectiveness.

Among the most expensive of these are the so-called 'Ching Pills' which contain a potent combination of yin and yang herbs especially formulated to nourish the internal organs and create extensive resources of energy. American author and herbalist Ron Teeguarden, who was taught by a Taoist master herbalist, reports that he has heard remarkable stories of rejuvenation from men who have used Ching Pills, and has personally experienced the powerful stimulating qualities of this deer velvet combination.

> The velvet extract is also widely used as a tonic to increase stamina and vitality. Ten drops under the tongue are taken daily or more often, as needed, to increase physical vigour and mental acuity. Pantocrin has been proven to be beneficial to metabolism, to the heart, central nervous system and brain, to the reproductive system, and as a general tonic after childbirth.[13]

Another herbal velvet antler formula is described by American herbalist Dr Michael Tierra as one of the most powerful energy tonics for men and women of all ages.

> It raises body metabolism and treats symptoms of coldness, poor digestion, weakness, aging, arthritic and rheumatic complaints and poor memory. It is also good for weak and sickly children, infants who are not growing, and lack of physical stamina. It is excellent for male and female hormone deficiencies, lack of sexual libido, frigidity and impotence.[14]

For medicinal purposes the velvet antler is divided roughly into four parts with the tips being the finest and most expensive part, containing the greatest concentration of growth hormones, and prescribed particularly for children and weakened people. The middle section has hemopoietic action and helps the heart and stomach. The next section down is said to relate to health, vigour and gynecologic disease, and is used in the treatment of arthritis and osteomyelitis; while the lower parts, being more mineralised, are said to be very effective for strengthening the bones (in calcium deficiency), particularly in the elderly.

In Oriental medicine the physical constitution of an individual is carefully studied before herbal formulas are prescribed. Traditionally the velvet is mixed with varying quantities of other herbs, depending on the patient's needs, which are then wrapped into small packages and taken home to prepare. This usually involves long periods of boiling or simmering until the tonic is ready, an aspect of Oriental medicine that has often turned Westerners away from the benefits to be found in this ancient tradition.

Although it is undoubtedly one of the most valuable remedies, velvet antler may be contraindicated for severe headache, influenza, serious liver, kidney or heart disease. However, in all of the documentation available there are no reported cases of toxic overdose or poisoning. Nosebleeds or headaches may occur if the dosage is too high, but by all accounts, from the very young to the very old, men and women have safely taken velvet antler for thousands of years.

To list all of the therapeutic claims made for velvet antler is far beyond the scope of this book, and the examples given here are but a tantalising slice of its extraordinary medicinal history paralleled by few other known herbal substances. While Asians continue to use it in the traditional way, other more convenient forms of velvet and velvet extracts are beginning to appear on the market, more suited perhaps to a modern and busier world, a world where there is no longer time to quietly simmer a pot of herbs on the stove for hours.

But although traditions change, the potency of velvet, 'the

greatest source of yang energy' will always be highly valued in Oriental medicine, and as its attributes become better known abroad many Westerners will surely become converts to this wonderfully safe and natural remedy.

NOTES

1. Fulder, Stephen, *The Book of Ginseng and other Chinese Herbs for Vitality*, p139, Healing Arts Press, Rochester, Vermont
2. Yoon, Dr Peter, *Guide to Deer Velvet*, New Zealand Game Industry Board
3. Wong, Samson C.S., of the Tak Tai Ginseng Firm Ltd, Hong Kong, *It's in their blood*, an edited version of an address at the Second International Wildlife Ranching Symposium in Edmonton, published in *The Deer Farmer*, September 1990
4. Holmes, Peter, *Jade Remedies: A Chinese Herbal Reference for the West*, Snow Lotus Press, Boulder (1997)
5. Teeguarden, Ron, *Chinese Herbal Tonics*, Cha Yuan Press, California (1991) p.69
6. Worsley, J. R., *Acupuncture—Is it for You?*, Element Books Limited, Dorset, England (1988)
7. "A 2000 Year Old Medicine from Deer Antlers," *New Health and Medical Findings from Around the World*, Life Extension Magazine, Vol.14, No. 12, December 1994. pp. 99-103
8. Archer, Dr. R. H., and Palfreyman, P. J., *Properties of New Zealand Deer Velvet*, Part I, Search of the Literature, Vol 1, for Massey University and Wrightson NMA Ltd. (1983)
9. ibid.
10. ibid.
11. ibid.
12. Yoon, Dr. Peter, *The Medical Effect of Deer Velvet*, a paper presented to the New Zealand Deer Farmers' Conference, 1995
13. Teeguarden, op. cit. p.165
14. Tierra, Dr. Michael, *Planetary Herbology*, Lotus Press, Santa Fe, New Mexico (1988) p.143

Medicinal benefits from NZ velvet antler

Evidence of the medical benefits of deer velvet antler is growing, according to AgResearch Invermay scientist Dr

Diagnostic tests are being developed to detect the presence of velvet antler in powders or extracts of unknown origin.

This is the first time such research has been carried in a western country. Velvet antler is typically used as a tonic to western being in Korea. AgResearch

2000 years of Tradition proved to be true

New Zealand Scientists have proved what oriental medicine has known for more than 200 years that it used for a preventative treatment in its own right and to support some remedial treat-

in the international natural health market," Mr Christie said.

The New Zealand deer industry organisation, the New Zealand Game Industry Board (NZGIB), commissioned AgResearch tonic especially

dustry is now developing industry quality and efficacy standards for velvet products, based on these scientific tests. Traditionally, velvet is used in Asia as a nourishing

"curing illness" philosophy, on which oriental medicine is based. Treatment with New Zealand velvet extract, at varying levels of strength, consistently produced this re-

Sporting success a boost to velvet

WELLINGTON — The use of deer velvet to boost stamina and strength in at been given a fillip by rece

New Zea who has bee land deer ve performanc held off all tain his p strongest r

His tim 2000m race at the wor championships was a f second outside the wor set last year and is a psychological advantag ing his single sculls titl

In the women's even Caroline and Georg Swindell, who are also t the deer velvet trial.

Proof NZ deer velvet has healing powers

By Neal Wallace

Scientists at Ag Research Invermay have proved what oriental doctors have known for more than 2000 years – deer velvet has health benefits.

Joint research carried out by scientists at Invermay and Otago University shows that treating human white-blood cells with extracts of New Zealand antler velvet stimulates the immune system, measured by increased production of white cells.

Ag Research Invermay scientist Dr Jimmy Suttie said the findings proved New Zealand velvet had the same medicinal qualities as higher-priced Russian and Chinese velvet.

In many Asian countries tonic, which includes velvet extract, is fed to children in and early winter to

They received an enthusiastic response, which he said should help stop the slide in New Zealand velvet prices in a market awash with an over supply of velvet.

"If the Game Industry Board and Ag Research had not stepped in and done this research, New Zealand velvet antler could have been worst off in terms of export

Velvet's benefits proven

DUNEDIN — Scientists at Ag-Research Invermay have proven what Oriental doctors have known for more than 2000 years — that deer velvet has health benefits.

Joint research by scientists at Invermay and the University of Otago showed that treating human white blood cells with extracts of New Zealand antler velvet stimulated the immune system, measured by In many Asia

strengthening the body's immune system. A spin-off could also be a raised profile for New Zealand's $50-million annual velvet exports in key markets such as Korea and Taiwan, said Mr Christie.

AgResearch Invermay scientist Dr Jimmy Suttie said the findings proved New Zealand velvet had the same medicinal qualities as Russian and Chinese

Korean pharmacists in a series of seminars in Korea and Taiwan.

"We presented the data on the efficacy of New Zealand velvet with the clear intention of preventing them from coming up with an excuse that New Zealand velvet is not effective," he said.

Chinese cures tailored for modern market

BEIJING — For centuries Chinese doctors have prescribed herbal mixes to be boiled up at home to help cure or prevent illnesses.

But in the modern Chinese world of long work days, fast food and widely available Western-style drugs, herbal companies are scrambling to find new formats for traditional medicines that are more convenient.

The traditional method of brewing

trained in Western medicine who also uses Chinese herbal remedies. "Kids won't touch it."

New Metabolife, a California-based maker of a dietary supplement for weight loss, has started a venture in Beijing to market Chinese herbal cures in tablet form in the United States and China.

"Our company sees Chinese traditional medicine as its future," said Michael Ellis, the company's founder

supplements, particularly herbal ones, and the US Food and Drug Administration leaves the market alone, unless a supplement proves hazardous or is marketed as a drug.

Other American companies are searching China for more herbal products to sell. Pharmanex is importing red yeast powders from China and marketing it in the United States as a cholesterol-cutting-product.

4

SCIENTIFIC RESEARCH RESULTS

With the results that are expected from scientific research, it is likely that velvet will become as accepted in Western countries as vitamins and other dietary supplements.[1]

While the therapeutic claims for antler velvet are well established in traditional Oriental medicine, velvet's reputation as a remedy for many health problems is also growing in the West. As medical costs soar and industrial and biological pollutants invade our food and water sources people are turning to natural remedies in ever increasing numbers, especially as the damaging side effects of many chemical drugs are now becoming apparent.

Today the natural health business in the United States is a multi-billion dollar industry. Ancient tonic herbs such as ginseng, reishi, and royal jelly are reestablishing themselves as highly effective immune boosting tonics and among these elite, newly rediscovered remedies is deer antler velvet, which, according to *Life Extension Magazine* "...is poised to be one of the most versatile multipurpose natural remedies to arrive in the West".[2]

But what is the scientific evidence behind such claims as this? While velvet antler can only be sold as a 'dietary supplement' under existing health regulations, there is intense interest in the results of scientific tests which are proving what Oriental doctors have taken as a matter of course for thousands of years.

Since 1991, New Zealand scientists have been carrying out a unique investigation into the composition and medical properties of velvet at AgResearch Invermay, near Dunedin in the South Island. The research was commissioned by Velvet Antler Research New Zealand (VARNZ), a joint venture between AgResearch and the New Zealand Game Industry Board (NZGIB) in association with the Universities of Canterbury and Otago.

THE COMPOSITION OF VELVET ANTLER

While extensive research has been carried out in Russia where velvet antler has been used clinically for decades, China, Korea and Japan, this was the first time such research has been carried out in a Western country. The first stage of the project was directed into the actual growth and composition of antlers. Their extraordinary rapid growth means that the chemical composition is constantly changing and it also varies within the antler itself, a fact that is well known to Oriental practitioners who classify each part of the antler separately from the tip to the base.

They call the tip the wax piece or *lu pian,* and it has the texture and colour of honey. It is also the most expensive section. The upper part is called *xie pian,* or blood piece, the next section down is called *feng pian,* which refers to its honeycomb appearance, and the base is the bone section or *gu pian.*

To study New Zealand velvet in comparison with the Russian and Chinese—traditionally regarded as the world's best—both young and mature red deer, wapiti and fallow deer antlers were analysed. After being dried and weighed each antler was divided into four sections and the ash, mineral and lipid (or fat) content was measured. While the mineral content of the antlers were similar, the lipid content of New Zealand red and fallow velvet was found to be higher than the Russian maral and Chinese malu. It is in the lipid, or fat, that the valuable active ingredients of velvet are found, and a higher lipid content signifies a correspondingly higher potency.

During the analysis, many of the major minerals needed to maintain healthy bodies were found to be present including calcium, phosphorus, sulphur, magnesium, potassium, sodium, manganese, zinc, copper, iron, selenium and cobalt. As would be expected, the calcium levels were found to be lowest in the tip, and increased towards the base as the calcification increased. On the other hand, the lipid content was highest in the tip, the most valuable section of the antler, and decreased in the lower portions.

There were also marked differences noted depending on the stage of antler growth, with the older antlers showing an increased content of ash, calcium and phosphorus, and decreased amounts of lipid, sulphur, sodium, potassium and selenium.

Every one of the minerals and trace elements found in velvet antler contribute in some way to a healthy immune system and these minerals alone, quite apart from any other bioactive substances, could help to explain its value in the treatment of osteoporosis, anaemia and as a growth stimulant for children.

Also found in velvet in varying quantities are a wide range of bioactive properties. These include: amino acids, collagen, polyamines, androgens, estrogens, ectosaponins, mucopolysaccharides, glucosamines, hematopoietin, glucosaminoglycans, N-Acetyl-glucosamine, chondroitin sulfate A, anti-inflammatory prostaglandins, erythropoietin (a glycoprotein produced in the kidney that stimulates red blood cell production in the bone marrow), and gangliosides (believed to be involved with cell metabolism and growth).

Found mainly in the central nervous system but also in other tissues, gangliosides consist of fatty acids, sphingosine, simple sugars, galactosamine and sialic acid. The sphingomyelins are "involved in complex bioregulatory pathways", they are believed to be biologically active and are possibly very important for the quality of the velvet. Once again the highest levels were found in the antler tips and the lowest in the base as the antler became more mineralised.[3]

The antler also contains fibroblasts and chondroblasts— the cells from which connective tissue and cartilage are developed; chondro- and osteocytes— cartilage and bone cells; growth factors including IGF-1 and IGF-2, and epidermal and nerve growth factors.

Also analysed were the concentrations of free amino acids, the basic building blocks of protein that are essential for healthy cell growth. While all twenty-two amino acids are manufactured by plants through the process of photosynthesis, humans and animals are able to synthesize all but a few amino acids, called 'essential' because they must be supplied ready-made through the food we eat.

Tests show that velvet antler contains all eight essential amino acids. It is composed primarily of protein, with collagen as the major protein consisting of glycine, alanine, proline and hydroxyproline. Amino acids found in other velvet proteins include: tryptophan, lysine, threonine, valine, leucine, isoleucine, phenylalanine, histidine, arginine, spartic acid, serine, glutamic acid, cysteine, methionine, and tyrosine.

These amino acids form patterns of concentration throughout the antlers, with the level of some being higher in the tips, and others more strongly concentrated in the base but overall, the levels of most amino acids were significantly higher in the higher graded velvet.

While the first stage of the Invermay research project has

firmly established New Zealand velvet as among the best in the world, comparing favourably with the traditional sources from China and Russia, the second and more extensive stage involves providing the scientific and clinical data necessary for velvet to be accepted as a medicine by Western health authorities.

VERIFYING ANCIENT CLAIMS

Today, clinical and scientific research using the extract of velvet antler is proving the validity of claims made by traditional medicine. The groundbreaking work carried out by AgResearch into the benefits of velvet is attracting attention from around the world and the research results are showing this ancient remedy to be one of nature's safest multipurpose energy tonics.

Evidence of the medical benefits of velvet antler is growing, according to Dr Jimmy Suttie, leader of the scientific team which is coming up with some exciting discoveries, and world expert on deer velvet research.[4] The trials so far have concentrated on testing extracts of velvet antler on growth, endurance and stamina, immunology, anti-inflammatory and anti-cancer activity.

Results from these trials have shown that treating human white blood cells with extracts of velvet antler stimulated the immune system, as measured by increased production of white blood cells. This response—*immunopotentiation* in scientific terms—is the body's defence mechanism, as increased numbers of white blood cells are produced to fight infection. Treatment with velvet, from varying parts of the antler, consistently produced a powerful response.[5]

Velvet antler has also demonstrated potent anti-inflammatory and growth stimulating properties.

Research is presently being carried out in Korea using velvet antler in conjunction with cancer therapies and while a great deal of work remains to be done, the results of these tests carry major implications for Western medicine with the very real probability of velvet being prescribed in mainstream therapies, both as a preventative and to support some remedial cancer treatments.

As the Game Industry Board's former chief executive Rick Christie said, "There is extensive anecdotal evidence of velvet's effectiveness, but now we're generating some rational scientific evidence to verify those claims. That's an important step for velvet in the international natural health market."

Further trials carried out by AgResearch testing athletes for increased muscular strength and endurance has also had very encouraging results, reflecting previous research carried out in Russia, and giving evidence as to the effectiveness of the velvet antler extracts used in Soviet Olympic training programs.

At the forefront of research in New Zealand and abroad has been the development of commercial deer velvet extracts in which the biologically and clinically active substances are highly concentrated. Since the 1930s, Russian scientists have developed and extensively tested the extract known as pantocrin. To obtain pantocrin the dried, crushed velvet undergoes a series of alcohol extractions and is then filtered and dried, forming a yellow crystalline substance. The pantocrin is then used medicinally in three forms, as a liquid alcohol extract, as a solution for injections, and as tablets. The extract from reindeer velvet, known as rantarin, is also widely used as a medicinal preparation throughout Russia.

"Very little of the ash, nitrogen, phosphorus or protein is extracted from the antlers in the preparation of pantocrin. Conversely, most of the fat in the antler is extracted into pantocrin... Hence, pantocrin is essentially the lipid fraction of velvet antlers."[6] And, as mentioned previously, it is in the lipid that the valuable active ingredients are found.

Long before velvet antler had stirred any interest in the Western scientific world, Russian researchers were carrying out some interesting studies of their own into the major remedies of Oriental medicine. At the Institute of the Physiology and Pharmacology of Adaptation, Vladivostok, Professor Israel I. Brekhman and colleagues had begun a systematic exploration of over one hundred traditional Chinese remedies, noting the combination of herbal and other substances used in the recipes, their active components, and how the medicines were prepared and taken.[7]

Among the great variety of herbal formulas Brekhman analysed, most were composed of the roots and leaves of various plant species, with ginseng, the 'king of herbs', heading the list. But also standing out among the few animal remedies listed were young deer antlers, otherwise known as velvet antler, or the Russian *pantui*.

It was due to Brekhman's further research into the pharmacological properties of ginseng that the wall of superstition and mystery surrounding Chinese medicine was penetrated, slowly but surely changing the attitude of the Western world towards this ancient system of health. Today, of course, ginseng is universally known and freely available from health food stores and even supermarkets across the world. It has become one of the best selling herbs on the American natural healthcare market.

However, the research of Brekhman and Professor S. M. Pavlenko into deer antler velvet is not so well known, although several volumes of medical studies on velvet have been produced in Russia over the past fifty years, mostly originating from the Institute of Biologically Active Substances in Vladivostock. Brekhman's tests for the pharmacological activity of velvet were adopted as a standard quality test for velvet antler, and in 1962, pantocrin was approved for general sale by the Ministry of Health. Since that time it has been widely prescribed and taken by thousands of people in Russia, and its effects have been carefully documented.[8]

The extensive body of scientific literature from Russia, as well as Korea and China, proves and supports the traditional use of velvet antler.

In particular Russian studies using pantocrine, an alcohol/water extract, have shown that velvet antler has hypotensive, erythropoietic, anti-stress, stimulating, anti-inflammatory, gonadotrophic, growth and metabolic effects.[9]

Pantocrin's use as a tonic in cases of mental and physical strain, hypertension, neuroses, sexual weakness and anaemia is endorsed by the Ministry of Public Health of the Russian Federation.

It is routinely used to treat such physical disorders as stomach ulcers, chronic gastritis, hepatitis and cerebral arteriosclerosis, and for the mental disorders schizophrenia and epilepsy. Russian practice is to administer the extract in diluted form—25 to 40 drops in water twice a day as part of a two to three week course.[10]

While the Russians have been convinced of velvet's high therapeutic efficacy for decades, Western health authorities demand hard scientific and clinical data before there is any chance of velvet becoming accepted as a medicine. But already a large body of literature exists which documents the pharmacological effects of velvet, and in the following pages we will take a closer look at these fascinating areas of research.

NOTES

1. Velvet Information Sheet from the NZ Game Industry Board.

2. *A 2000 Year Old Medicine from Deer Antlers* New Health and Medical Findings from Around the World, Life Extension Magazine: Vol. 14, No. 12, December 1994, pp.99-103

3. Suttie, J.M. et al., *The New Zealand Velvet Antler Industry: Background and Research Finding*, International Symposium on Cervi Parvum Cornu, The Korean Society of Pharmacognosy, Seoul, Korea, 1994

4. *Medicinal benefits from New Zealand velvet antler*, AgResearch Invermay, 3 November, 1997.

5. *2000 Years of Tradition Proved to be True*, Media Release, NZ Game Industry Board, Wellington, September, 1997

6. Archer, Dr R.H. and Palfreyman, P.J., *Properties of New Zealand Deer Velvet*, Part I, Search of the Literature, Volume 1, for Massey University and Wrightson NMA Ltd (1983)

7. Fulder, Stephen, *The Book of Ginseng and other Chinese Herbs for Vitality*, p139, Healing Arts Press, Rochester, Vermont (1980)

8. ibid.

9. Suttie, Dr James M and Haines, Stephen R., *Evaluation of New Zealand Velvet Antler Efficacy and Diagnostic Testing*, AgResearch, Invermay Agricultural Centre, Mosgiel (1997)

10. *Glenalbany: Tapping the remarkable secrets of pantocrin*, Deer Antler Velvet, updated edition June 1994, The Deer Farmer/Game Industry Board, Wellington.

Grading velvet slices for the Asian market.

5

THERAPEUTIC BENEFITS OF VELVET ANTLER

...all experimental and clinical investigations give concerted testimony to the fact that pantocrin is a rather valuable medicine. If one selects from all the variety of its pharmacological effects the main ones, these, undoubtedly, are the stimulating, tonic, and gonadotrophic effects, as well as the capacity to raise the general non-specific resistance of the organism. Brekhman[1]

POWERFUL TONIC EFFECTS

In the Western world today countless people suffer from the effects of chronic fatigue, tiredness and low vitality. It could almost be called the plague of twentieth century existence, waking in the morning feeling sluggish, seeming never to have the energy we would like to get everything done and then falling into bed at night exhausted. To combat this lack of energy we pour another cup of coffee which works in the short term, but with long term use stimulants such as caffeine deplete the body's energy resources even further.

Perhaps the most insidious energy thief, apart from bad diet and lack of exercise, is stress. According to American author Dr Pelletier, stress related illnesses "have become the number one social and health problem in the last decade."[2] Continuous stress undermines the body's natural defences and weakens the immune system with the resulting disease and debilitating illness, from heart attacks and strokes to the symptoms of chronic fatigue syndrome.

As resistance to disease is controlled by the immune system, any remedies that work to strengthen this defensive system are becoming much in demand, and with the results of New Zealand scientific research backing up the claims of traditional Chinese medicine, velvet antler can now take its place in Western healthcare as one of nature's most effective immune boosting supplements.

Doctor of pharmacology, Stephen Fulder, has extensively explored the healing properties of the Chinese 'kingly remedies' and describes velvet antler as belonging in the category of what he calls harmony drugs. As he says, "It has no apparent effect in the absence of stress, but as soon as stress is applied it restores body processes to normal... In other words, the stress sets the drugs working, and the body's general resistance is increased."[3]

To stimulate the system without robbing it of energy is a subject of vital interest to health practitioners, and as information on the uses and properties of Chinese herbs becomes more freely available this interest has become particularly focused on those substances referred to as 'tonics' in the Chinese pharmacopeia. As tonic is a somewhat vague description, the term 'adaptogen' has been coined, meaning that the function of these remedies is to increase the body's ability to adapt to the environment, to adapt physically and mentally to the changes and stresses of life. They are the herbs that promote inner vitality and energy while increasing the body's resistance to stress and disease. Among these, velvet antler has always been regarded as one of the finest to be found.

As Ron Teeguarden notes in his book on tonic herbs:

> Many people in the West who had previously used stimulants such as coffee, amphetamines, or cocaine have switched to the harmless Pantocrin for quick substantial energy. Pantocrin has been found to be a healthful central nervous system stimulant.[4]

At Ron's exclusive Tea Garden Herbal Emporium in Malibu, California, the rejuvenating properties of Chinese herbs are becoming sought after by the rich and famous. Actor Mel Gibson swears by the efficacy of tonic herbal formulas, and "Mel's Punch", held to be "the ultimate health cocktail", contains deer antler, herbs and mushrooms and costs $20 a thimbleful.[4a]

While Hollywood stars spread the word about their costly rejuvenating formulas, a great deal of research into many of these traditional herbs has been carried out in Russia. Studies focusing on the effects of velvet antler extract in clinical testing have shown an overwhelming recurring theme—that it has a powerful tonic and revitalising effect on the individual, especially on a person weakened in any way by stress or illness. It is in this capacity that velvet antler seems bound to play an important role in the future.

Fulder writes:

> Pantocrin has for years been regularly administered to promote patient recovery in Soviet hospitals and clinics, the earliest clinical reports appearing in the 1930s. It too is found useful in promoting recovery and a restoration of health in convalescents, undernourished and tubercular children, and those weakened by chronic diseases.

He goes on to say,

> Professor Albov, for example, has tested it extensively in patients who were one degree under for some time after diseases such as viral infections or dysentery. He notes a restoration of blood pressure, improved mood, digestion, stamina and body weight. He also recounts

his experience of the use of pantocrine in helping soldiers with serious war-wounds to return to health and strength.[5]

As research into the active constituents of velvet antler which endow it with such tremendous restorative powers are ongoing, the testimonials from people who have discovered its energy enhancing qualities fill the files of velvet antler producers in the West.

Experimental research has demonstrated that velvet preparations can protect the body from stress such as, heat, cold and electric shock. Russian studies cited by Dr Fennessy report that patients treated with velvet extract prior to surgery for gastrointestinal tumours had significantly lower levels of stress indicators in the blood.

According to another Russian researcher, Dr Korobkov, velvet extract acts "by accelerating the body's natural restorative processes and by increasing the body's resistance to unfavourable external influence."[6] In other experiments velvet antler helped to protect laboratory animals from liver damage by carbon tetrachloride.

IMPROVED ATHLETIC PERFORMANCE

Keen athletes and sports people should find the following information of more than passing interest. Although not widely known in the West, velvet antler in the form of pantocrin has been an essential part of Russian athletic training programmes for decades. In fact, the success of Russian athletes has been attributed to its use during Olympic training sessions.

In 1969, studies were carried out in Vladivostok to evaluate the traditional use of velvet in physical tests of stamina and endurance. In an experiment supervised by Dr Taneyeva, the test subjects began cycling on an ergonometer, which is a fixed bicycle with a workmeter attached. The men were then stopped and given either pantocrin or a placebo, and checked again two hours later. The pantocrin group showed a much greater increase in the total work achieved.[7]

In another experiment, again designed to test the endurance properties of velvet antler, fifty young men ran a three-kilometre race. The group that had been administered pantocrin thirty minutes before the race were considerably faster on average than the placebo group.

Studies similar to those of Dr Taneyeva, carried out in 1974 by Drs Yudin and Dobryakov, showed the performance of average healthy athletes improved considerably after being administered pantocrin. While control athletes on an exercise cycle performed 15 kg/meter of dynamic work, those given pantocrin increased this dramatically to 74 kg/m. Improved performance in running and weight-lifting were also documented.[8]

Not only a tonic for the body, velvet antler is also a powerful tonic for the mind as Dr Taneyeva discovered in 1964 when it was demonstrated that the mental capacity of young men improved significantly when they were given pantocrin before sitting down to a mathematical test.

The success of Russian athletes who have demonstrated a significant increase in endurance and muscular strength, has attracted the attention of sports doctors and trainers around the world who are seeking safe and natural alternatives to synthetic steroids. A fitness expert from the United States, John Abdo, who hosts a nationwide television fitness show, visited the Institute of Physical Culture in Moscow in 1989 to investigate Russian training routines. He came away convinced that deer velvet was a key factor in improving athletic performance; a non-toxic remedy for promoting strength, endurance, and swifter recuperation from injury.[9]

Dr Arkady Koltun, Chairman of the *Medical Committee for the Russian Bodybuilding Federation,* is one of the foremost Russian researchers into anabolic agents that can improve the performance of athletes. Working with kayakers, weightlifters, body-builders and power lifters, Dr Koltun found that deer velvet actually increases muscular strength—a property which is termed *myotropic.* He also found that it had potent nerve strengthening, or *neurotropic* properties and is beneficial in treating infectious diseases, fatigue and hypertension.[10]

Further research into velvet as an effective nutritional supplement for athletes during their training programmes is proving remarkably successful. A study at Otago University in New Zealand, designed to test the effect of deer velvet on athletic performance, was carried out in 1998 during a ten week project. Twenty four physical education students participated in this double blind trial, where neither the athletes nor the trial co-ordinator knew which treatment each group was receiving. The group taking the velvet showed almost *twice* the improvement of the group taking a placebo in the amount of work they were able to do in a strength test. Interestingly, the extra strength was discovered to come from improved muscle activity rather than increased muscle size.[11]

Dr Suttie, responsible for the scientific control of the study, noted that the group taking deer velvet had a similar level of body protein and fat as the control group, as shown by a sophisticated DEXA scanner.

> Contrary to popular misconception, the study showed that improving muscle strength does not necessarily require increasing muscle size. Scanning showed no bulking up of muscles, which suggested the positive results were due to an improvement in the muscle dynamic activity of the students taking deer velvet.[12]

In another study at the University of Otago designed to more closely investigate velvet's influence on building endurance and helping to repair injured muscle tissue, both vital issues for the competitive world of international sport, thirty athletes ran downhill on a treadmill to induce tissue damage in their thighs. Blood samples were then taken to measure the level of creatine kinase, a substance found in the bloodstream used as an indicator of muscle tissue damage. Those athletes who had been on a two week course of New Zealand velvet powder previously showed significantly reduced levels of creatine kinase in their blood.

Athletes taking the velvet also reported recovery from muscle soreness 24 hours earlier than the subjects receiving a placebo. Among the growing number of athletes who are discovering the benefits of deer velvet are triathlete Hamish Carter and rower Rob Waddell, both trialing New Zealand deer velvet as a safe and legal performance enhancer.

Hamish, who recently became the world's champion triathlete, said, "I really believe it helps my training, energy and endurance. I feel better and recover faster when taking velvet. I'm sure taking velvet has the potential to give me the incremental improvement all athletes strive for."[13]

World champion rower Rob Waddell also experienced a boost in stamina, strength and efficiency. "My strength in the gym has improved significantly," he said. "My ability to handle a higher load of training, and the level of my strength and physiology have been distinctly improved."[14]

Others taking part in trialing New Zealand deer velvet are also excelling in their chosen sports, such as Jannene Harker, World Champion Surf Life Saver who says, "My strength in the gym has increased...I have noticed a significant increase in not only the weight I am moving but on the eccentric phase of muscle contraction.

"Since taking deer velvet I have felt a sustained strength on the blade that has been missing in recent years. I can only put this down to deer velvet. I can definitely recommend deer velvet to anyone wishing to compete in sport or maintain a healthy lifestyle."[14a]

Another veteran who takes velvet daily is top golfer Bob Charles. At the British Open two years ago he said along with healthy eating habits and vitamins, two deer velvet capsules a day kept him feeling young. "I don't feel a day over 30," he said. "I'm 60, going on 30."[15]

By naturally boosting muscular strength and endurance, along with its excellent amino acid composition and mineral content, velvet antler may well be the future athlete's nutitional supplement of choice.

Anti-Inflammatory Properties
and Accelerated Wound Healing

In 1999, velvet antler was substantiated by clinical studies and scientific research, in compliance with the U.S. Food and Drug Administration, "to support healthy joint structure and function".

As many people will happily testify, one of the outstanding properties of velvet antler is its ability to alleviate the pain of inflammation, such as joint pain, swelling and tissue injury. While anti-inflammatories are widely prescribed in Western medicine for a large number of ailments, they can often cause severe and unpleasant side effects. In New Zealand pure velvet powder is widely taken to relieve the pain and symptoms of arthritis and has become popular among the elderly for this reason.

New Zealand velvet extract has shown strong anti-inflammatory effects in studies with mice (AgResearch, 1996),[15a] which are not due to cytotoxic acitivty. At this stage the reason for the effects are unknown.

It has been suggested that the high concentrations of hormone-like substances in deer velvet are responsible for the rapid tissue repair after injury, or even the cartilaginous concentration of the antler itself. When velvet antler is harvested it is still largely cartilage, containing such compounds as collagen and glycosaminoglycans (GAGs).

Research microbiologist Dr Alex Duarte, has spent many years researching the powerful healing properties of cartilage and in his book *The Benefits of Velvet Antler* he refers to studies that have been carried out using cartilage in the treatment of serious degenerative diseases.[16] In particular he refers to Dr John F. Prudden and other researchers who over thirty-five years ago discovered such elements in cartilage as N-Acetyl-Glucosamine, glycosaminoglycans and synoviocytes, all which have been associated with accelerated wound healing.

He describes glycosaminoglycans as being the "regulator of new cartilage production and turnover" and being "a very powerful regulator of synoviocytes, which regulate the integrity of the joint fluid."[17] He cites studies in which people suffering from severe osteoarthritis and rheumatoid arthritis showed overwhelmingly positive results when treated with bovine cartilage.

Glucosamine is formed from the combination of a sugar (glucose) and an amine, derived from the amino acid, glutamine. It is an important component in proteoglycans, which provide structure to the bones, cartilage, skin, nails, hair and other body tissues. It is essential for healthy cartilage and to maintain healthy joints and pain-free mobility.

The major GAG in velvet antler is chondroitin sulfate. Chondroitin is formed from a long chain of sugar molecules which helps to attract fluid into the proteoglycans. This is necessary to provide nutrients and lubrication into the joint cartilage which has no blood supply of its own. Termed "chondroprotective" agents, glucosamine and chondroitin are today being widely promoted to help rebuild cartilage and improve joint mobility in arthritis sufferers with very beneficial effects.

Duarte also cites Dr Lester Morrison, who over ten years ago observed chondroitin sulphate A to be an extremely powerful anti-inflammatory agent which reversed the degenerative condition of arteriosclerosis and dramatically improved circulation. He conducted a six-year study demonstrating that chondroitin sulphate A could reduce the incidence of fatal heart attack and stroke by over 400 percent just by daily oral consumption.

Further studies by Dr Prudden, involving the treatment of advanced cancer patients were also dramatic. There was a positive response from 90 percent of the patients and it was discovered that "cartilage protected the patients from the severe side effects of chemotherapy" apparently by protecting and strengthening the immune system.

While these studies have found cartilage to be a powerful anti-inflammatory and wound healing agent, the cartilage from velvet antler itself is unique as it contains many other bioactive compounds that are still under investigation. These include anti-inflammatory prostaglandins which play a role in reducing the swelling associated with tissue injury, arthritis, infection and pain. Research shows that velvet prostaglandins, which are unsaturated fatty acids, can induce vasodepression, smooth muscle contractions and also modulate lipid metabolism.

In other studies from Japan, velvet extract has been shown to speed up the healing of damaged nerve tissue, and also aids in the recovery of patients suffering from cervical and whiplash injuries.[18] Research has shown that long standing wounds and ulcers also respond well to velvet preparations, and the high level of phosphate, calcium and other minerals, as well as the growth hormone precursors, have been suggested as reasons why it is so effective in healing bones and wounds and helping with arthritic complaints.

The rapid yearly growth of antlers has provided a unique opportunity for the study of bone development by a research group at Lincoln University, Christchurch. The group has been studying the effect of the hormone oestradiol on antler tissue, in particular by activating receptors in the tissue which surrounds the antler bone beneath the skin.

Dr Graham Barrell writes, "Antlers are newly formed bones and the final burst of calcification depends on the secretion of sex hormones from the testes. Research at Lincoln and overseas has shown the hormone oestradiol is predominant in stimulating calcification of the antlers."[19] This on-going research may become very important for future work on the treatment of bone disorders such as osteoporosis.

BLOOD BUILDING AND REDUCTION OF BLOOD PRESSURE

According to modern research, velvet antler stimulates the production of blood by nourishing the bone marrow.

Velvet has long been recognized as being effective for increasing both the volume and the circulation of blood through the body. As a specific remedy in traditional medicine for anaemia it has been shown in experiments to have a potent erythropoetic effect, meaning that it stimulates the formation of red blood cells. Improving the oxygen carrying capacity of the blood and building the iron uptake of the red blood cells may account for its value in treating anaemia.

This "well-accepted erythropoietic activity"[20] which results in improved blood supply may also enhance muscle endurance and stamina both in athletes and in normal healthy people.

Reports from Korea showed that velvet extract increased the erythrocyte count and stimulated red blood cell synthesis in anaemic rabbits.[21] The rate of recovery of blood cell counts was faster in anaemic rabbits treated with elk or particularly New Zealand red deer velvet extracts. Experiments also showed that powdered velvet given orally or injected as preparations in rats increased the number of red and white blood cells, and large amounts resulted in a marked increase in the production of red blood cells.

In *Jade Remedies* we read that velvet antler increases "serum levels of erythrocytes, hemoglobin, leukocytes and reticulocytes" and also "promotes cellular rejuvenation through its ectosaponin content."[22]

While the tradition of women regularly taking tonics to nourish the blood is deeply ingrained in Asian culture, anaemia is very prevalent among women in the West. However, velvet antler could well become part of a new tradition as there are many reports of women taking velvet antler to increase the iron levels in their blood. For example, Dr Suttie recounts the story of a pregnant woman who was suffering from anaemia and took velvet antler. Within 48 hours her blood count was back to normal.[23]

Velvet not only builds blood but research has shown that it also has a strong influence on blood pressure—it lowers the arterial blood pressure, apparently due to its ability to increase the dilation of the peripheral blood vessels. This immediate lowering of blood pressure is a major property of velvet extract and since it is so easily demonstrated, is widely used as a test for its biological activity. It is interesting to note that while velvet extract has this marked hypotensive effect in normal people, it has also been shown to restore blood pressure to normal in both hypo- and hyper-tensive patients.

A Japanese study in which 8 out of 10 patients were given pantocrin resulted in significant and transient reductions in arterial blood pressure. The systolic reading was lowered by 20 to 70 points, and the diastolic by as much as 10 to 20mmHg. Taking into account all the objective and subjective indices, pantocrin was 80% effective.[23a]

Pharmacological and clinical research indicates that the use of deer velvet significantly improves the heart function, regulating hearts with arrhythmias and increasing the blood flow in subjects with chronically poor circulation.

The Russian researcher N.A. Albov studied the effects of injectable velvet extract on 13 patients with hypertension caused by heart disorders. After 20 days of injections examinations revealed that 84 percent of the patients had improved. In another trial of 32 patients with high blood pressure caused by obesity or early-onset menopause, after a course of velvet extract given orally or by injection 26 of the patients had measurably lower blood pressure.[23b]

ANABOLIC OR GROWTH STIMULATING PROPERTIES

For centuries children in Korea have been given velvet antler to promote their healthy growth and development, both physically and mentally. In a similar capacity, velvet has also been used as a strengthening tonic for invalids, and for patients suffering from chronic wasting diseases such as tuberculosis[24], AIDS,[25] and chronic fatigue syndrome.[26]

The nutrient rich, fast growing cartilage of deer antler velvet contains many growth factors that are under close investigation at AgResearch. During preliminary 'in vitro' studies, velvet extracts were found to not only stimulate cell growth, but also demonstrated anti-tumour and anti-viral properties.

During their investigations, the Invermay team measured a natural hormone called "insulin-like growth factor-1" or "IGF-1" among the natural growth hormones and their precursors found in velvet. High levels of this hormone were found in deer blood during the growth of the antlers, and "receptors to IGF-1" were found in the antler itself. Dr Suttie's group discovered that IGF-1 and a related hormone IGF-2, promoted growth in antler cells growing in the laboratory and more recent discoveries have shown that these antler cells are capable of producing IGF-2 themselves.

In the human body growth hormone is the most abundant hormone produced by the pituitary gland, and in the liver it triggers the release of IGF-1, also called somatomedin C. It is used by scientists as a measure for the level of growth hormone present in the body as it elicits most of the effects associated with growth hormone.

When we are young the concentration of human growth hormone is relatively high which promotes good musculature and low body fat. However after adolescence and during our early twenties, growth hormone levels decline along with IGF-1 and many studies have shown a direct correspondence between aging and a lack of growth hormone. As a natural source of IGF-1 it is claimed that the anabolic effect of deer velvet can help to keep the body lean by burning fat and building muscle tissue—of great interest to body builders, athletes, weight trainers, or any person wanting to keep in good shape.

In a recent breakthrough in velvet antler research a unique extract has been developed by a New Zealand company, Gold Mountain. This extract, standardised to the IGF-1 content yeilds pharmaceutical quality IGF-1 in a bioactive matrix containing insulin-like growth factors 1 and 2, transforming growth factors Alpha and Beta, epidermal growth factor, vascular endothelial growth factor, nerve growth factor, neurotrophin growth factor 3, fibroblast growth factors, interleukins, and bone morphogenetic protein 4.[26a]

The potential applications of this natural source of Cervine growth factor complex could transform the growth hormone industry.

The anabolic, or growth promoting effects of velvet antler have been well documented, and separate studies using mice,

tadpoles, chickens, young rabbits and rats have all shown stimulated growth and increased body weight.[27]

In a study carried out by AgResearch using New Zealand
velvet antler extract, healthy rats fed diets supplemented with
medium and high doses of velvet extract grew markedly more
than the control group, and their liver weight was also significantly heavier.[28] The rats fed with the highest level of extract
grew 12 percent heavier than the control group during the first
three weeks of the study.

Research by Dr Jeong Sim and Dr Hoon Sunwoo at the
University of Alberta has also demonstrated velvet's potent
growth-promoting effect, stimulating bone development in rats
by increasing femur length, thickness and mineral content.

Sexual Benefits

There is a very strong case for stating that ginseng and
pantocrine can increase sexual energy, and that they
would be a considerable help both to those who are
potent but sexually exhausted, and to those who are
impotent and wish they *could* be sexually exhausted.[29]

Velvet antler's reputation as an aphrodisiac is widespread, but is
this reputation deserved? After all, velvet along with herbal remedies such as ginseng, have been used by wealthy Asian men
for centuries as a sexual tonic to improve potency. Chinese
Taoists, for example, use an extensive array of herbal aphrodi-
siacs to increase sexual energy in the belief that it enhances
their overall health. They have a fundamental understanding
that the flow of sexual energy within the body is the basis of
physical and mental well being.

An aphrodisiac is defined as an agent that stimulates sexual
desire, however, velvet antler appears to have a much more
profound affect upon the organism than merely as a temporary
sexual stimulant. In traditional terms it is held to harmonize the
yin and *yang* energies, to bring the vital energies of the body
into balance at a deep and fundamental level. It appears to

affect the balance of hormones necessary for healthy sexual functioning, and to restore the body's reserves of energy depleted by stress or exhaustion. It is said to increase physical stamina and sexual vitality. As Fulder states:

"Sexual functions are controlled by the hypothalmic brain areas. Any agent, therefore, which can tune body functions hormonally would be expected to improve sexual energy."

The effects of velvet antler and pantocrin on patients with sexual disorders has been widely documented, especially by Russian clinical researchers, with the result that while ginseng used to be famous for treating sex problems in Russian clinics, now pantocrin has taken over for this purpose.[30] It is regarded as one of the most effective known remedies for impotence. It increases the libido and the general sexual function, and is widely prescribed for women as well as men.

In *Jade Remedies* velvet antler is reported to be "used for incontinence, sexual disinterest, impotence, infertility."

Research has shown that velvet antler demonstrates androgenic and gonadotrophic effects, meaning that it increases the production of testosterone and its metabolites and helps to regulate the activity of the sex organs. A series of investigations by Pavlenk et al. (1969) has shown that pantocrin contains biologically active substances of both the male and female sex hormone types.

The sex hormones estrone, testosterone and a substance similar to progesterone have been identified at low levels in velvet, and the estrogen hormone most affected by velvet is estradiol, which is a precursor to testosterone. Also found by New Zealand scientists is a hormone called lutinizing hormone (LH) which is secreted by the pituitary gland and is the testosterone master-hormone, giving the signal for testosterone to be produced in the body.

Experimentally, velvet has been shown to boost testosterone and estrogen levels in rats, and according to modern research, it can stimulate growth and increase the weight of both the seminal vesicles and prostate.

When ginseng, eleutherococcus, rantarin (reindeer antler velvet) or pantocrine were given continuously to young male mice, the weight of their sexual glands increased by up to 50 per cent, depending on the preparation and the dose...Only pantocrine and rantarin had a measurable effect in mature as well as immature animals.[31]

Also, perhaps as an unexpected side effect:

Rantarin treatment of arteriosclerotic patients led some to recover sexual functioning and experience a return of potency and libido. [32]

Velvet's value in treating impotence is well known in traditional Oriental medicine and is widely used for that purpose in China. Dr Shi Zhi Chou, a specialist in men's sexual problems from Dalian Traditional Chinese Medical Hospital, lists some 300 formulas in his book *The Most Effective Prescriptions For Impotence*. Velvet antler is listed in almost every one of them.

There are many anecdotal accounts on file from men who having taken antler velvet to increase energy, or to lower blood pressure, or alleviate the pain of arthritis, have enjoyed the bonus of greatly increased sexual interest and capacity. Velvet builds endurance, it seems, on every level.

Among the volumes of documented research into the therapeutic benefits of velvet antler from Russia, China, Korea and Japan, many reports relate directly to its sexual benefits:

According to Dr Kong (1980) of the Chinese University of Hong Kong...Velvet preparations increase muscle tone, increase lung efficiency and increase appetite. It acts like a male sex hormone, animal tests showing it to be about half the strength of testosterone.

Nikitina (1974) claims that in the East [velvet antler] is considered as a means ...for the heightening of the sexual function.

Wallnofer and von Rattausher (1975) In their book 'Chinese Folk Medicine and Acupuncture' claim that deer antlers... are an excellent excitant for men whose sexual potency is declining.

Rennie (1980) when discussing the deer industry in Taiwan said that, as elsewhere, velvet antler is considered a general tonic and body rejuvenator, particularly good for... boosting sexual performance in men.[32a]

VELVET FOR WOMEN

While velvet antler extract is regarded as the ultimate primal tonic for men, it is also widely prescribed in Russia for women, especially for treating menstrual problems and alleviating the symptoms of menopause.

Western medicine, particularly in the United States, promotes the use of hormonal replacement therapy (HRT) for women at menopause, which involves giving small doses of oestrogen to women in order to compensate for the dramatic drop in the amount of oestrogen being produced by the ovaries. It is a very controversial therapy, with studies showing that in the short term HRT may banish the debilitating effects of menopause but as reports show, it may unleash greater health risks such as thrombosis and uterine cancer later in life.

Women seeking less invasive ways to balance the hormonal system during menopause, which can be a time of intense physical and psychological stress, may be interested to know that in Russia pantocrin and rantarin are officially recommended for menopausal problems, as well as for delayed and abnormal menstrual cycles.

Fulder states, "Pantocrine was found very useful in reduced sexual function and menopausal disorders of circulation; in depression and psychological problems, and pain in the joints." He goes on to say that some of the menopausal women treated in this way even started menstruating again.[33]

According to Brekhman

A number of reports particularly stressed the therapeutic effect of pantocrin in various kinds of sexual disorders in men and women, especially associated with climacteric syndrome.

Women taking velvet have reported diminished symptoms of pre-menstrual syndrome, even to the point where periods pass by almost unnoticed. They have also reported heightened sexual interest, an intensity of erotic dreams, and a sense of being in touch with deeper reserves of vital energy.

While pantocrin given to young male mice caused an increase in the size of their sexual glands, similar experiments were carried out in Russia by Brekhman and Taneyeva to investigate the gonadotrophic action of velvet extract on female mice. During these experiments they discovered an increase in the weight of the uterus and ovaries of the mice, and also an increased number of oestrus cycles.[34]

Whether the effect is on male or female, velvet appears to have a profound strengthening and balancing influence upon the hormonal system. As Teeguarden states, "pantocrin has been proven to be beneficial to metabolism, to the heart, central nervous system and brain, to the reproductive system."

For thousands of years women in China have traditionally been prescribed velvet antler for infertility and "female reproductive debility." They take it to increase fertility, then during pregnancy to ensure the health of mother and baby. They are given velvet during childbirth to aid in the baby's delivery, and after childbirth as a general tonic to increase lactation and restore and rejuvenate the mother's energy and health. In combination with herbal blood tonics such as dong quai, velvet is an invaluable addition to the woman's pharmacopeia.

ANTI-AGING EFFECTS

The elderly in Asia take velvet during the cold winter months, when the body is most vulnerable to infection and disease. It is traditionally said to benefit a wide variety of mental and physical health processes that are involved with aging, including strengthening the mind and increasing the quality and length of life. Its positive influence is so marked that Brekhman distinguishes pantocrin from all other adaptogens because its effects are "manifest with particular distinction in elderly and old people."

The revitalising effects of velvet antler have long been known in Oriental medicine and well documented in Russian clinical trials where both pantocrin and rantarin are used to treat the elderly. "In Russia where eleutherococcus and particularly pantrocrine/rantarin are given to the elderly, many trials have been reported," writes Fulder. "In one study using elderly patients with some degree of atherosclerosis, rantarin was found to improve sleep, memory, mood and drive, and to alleviate headaches."[35]

More recent research carried out by Chinese scientist Wang Benxiang and associates suggests that velvet preparations showed anti-aging effects by reducing signs of senility in mice. They found a big increase in plasma testosterone concentrations in the treated mice; they had far less oxidation by-product in their liver and brains, and free radical scavenger activity was greater than in the control mice.(Wang et al., 1988)

It was also discovered that the velvet treatment significantly inhibited MAO enzyme function (monoamine oxidase), an enzyme which breaks down certain neurotransmitters in the brain, like serotonin, dopamine, and norepinephrine. As people age, MAO activity increases, breaking down these neurotransmitters too quickly. The mood and energy enhancing effects of velvet antler on the elderly may lie in its MAO-inhibiting action.

In fact, velvet has traditionally been used to treat many of the health problems described today as characteristic of growth hormone deficiency. In *Growth Hormone: Reversing Human Aging Naturally* pharmacologist James Jamieson observes:

> The decline of growth hormone with age, sometimes referred to as somatopause, is directly associated with many of the symptoms of aging, including wrinkles, grey

hair, decreased energy and sexual funtion, increased body fat and cardiovascular disease, osteoporosis, and more... The good news is that clinical evidence demonstrates that by replacing growth hormone we can dramatically reverse these symptoms.[35a]

As a natural source of IGF-1 and growth hormone precursors, velvet antler may well act as a key for the body to naturally stimulate its own production of growth hormone in the pituitary. Unlike other growth hormone products available in the booming anti-aging industry velvet is neither the glandular extract of a dead animal, nor is it the product of recombinant DNA technology (genetic engineering). Velvet is a naturally safe tonic proven effective by countless generations of elderly Asian people.

Anti-Cancer and AIDS

While there is no evidence to date showing that velvet antler actually cures cancer, experiments carried out in Russia have shown extracts to increase the survival rate and, in some instances, to inhibit the spread of tumour cells in rats and mice.[36]

To determine whether the extracts of New Zealand velvet antler are effective in anti-cancer treatments, AgResearch has been running clinical trials in Korea and according to Dr Suttie the first series of experiments have shown positive results.

A major problem with the drugs used in chemotherapy is the damage they cause to the body while destroying the cancer cells. However, it was discovered during experiments that the aqueous extracts of velvet antler increased the effectiveness of the anti-cancer drugs while at the same time reducing their side effects. They were clearly potent at reducing the damaging side effects of the anti-cancer drug, in particular by reducing damage to the kidneys.[37]

As New Zealand GIB chief executive Rick Christie said, "We're not saying that deer velvet is a cure for cancer, Aids or any other complaint. But the science strongly indicates that deer velvet may be effective in supporting other treatments."[38]

Recovery of weight was greatest in the mice treated with the aqueous extract of velvet antler, which normalised or partly normalised spleen, kidney and liver weight.

As an immune enhancer for patients with AIDS, velvet is mentioned in *Jade Remedies*. It is also listed as an ingredient in a formula for people with HIV which is under study at the Institute for Traditional Medicine in Long Beach, California. It is hoped that the formula will help the bone marrow and increase white blood cells, red cells, and T-helper counts.

There is also evidence that velvet antler reduces cholesterol levels, as demonstrated by Soshnianina (1974), whose experiments showed a reduction of liver, spleen and brain cholesterol in guinea pigs under the influence of velvet extract.[39] In contrast kidney cholesterol was increased leading the author to conclude that the extract was causing the cholesterol to be filtered from the blood thus increasing kidney levels but lowering levels elsewhere in the body.

Pantrocrin is also used for treating epilepsy and, according to Fulder, it has been widely recommended in Russia for treating this condition. It was reported by Brekhman that the depressive states and psychoses associated with epilepsy "could be arrested by pantocrin considerably sooner than by other methods of treatment."[40]

Other conditions reported to be alleviated or cured by velvet extract include skin disease such as excema and psoriasis, infected and slow healing wounds—as it promotes the granulation of tissue—as well as bone fractures.

Considering velvet antler's long history of use in Chinese medicine as an ingredient of formulas prescribed for a wide range of human ailments, together with the extensive Russian literature available on pantocrin's clinical testing and the ongoing research being carried out in the West, particularly in the area of growth hormone therapy, it will be highly interesting to see how the role of this extraordinary supplement evolves in Western medicine and natural health care.

Although many of velvet antler's secrets have yeilded to the scrutiny of scientists, there are components as yet unidentified and unknown. As Dr. Suttie says: "We may find velvet contains only the raw material for a therapeutic activity. But, it is also possible that subtle combinations of active ingredients create synergistic acitivity that makes velvet a healing medicine."[41]

NOTES

1. Archer, Dr. R. H., and Palfreyman, P. J., *Properties of New Zealand Deer Velvet*, Part I, Search of the Literature, Vol 1, for Massey University and Wrightson NMA Ltd. (1983)

2. Fulder, Stephen, *The Book of Ginseng and other Chinese Herbs for Vitality*, p.180, Healing Arts Press, Rochester, Vermont (1980)

3. ibid. p.162

4. Teeguarden, Ron, *Chinese Tonic Herbs*, p.124, Japan Publications, Inc, Tokyo and New York, (1985)

4a. New Zealand *New Idea* magazine, June 1998

5. Fulder op. cit. p.198

6. Archer and Palfreyman op. cit.

7. ibid.

8. ibid.

9. Duarte, Alex, *The benefits of Velvet Antler: The 2000-Year-Old Health Food For All Reasons*, 1995

10. ibid

11. Gerrard, D.F. et al., *Clinical Evaluation Of New Zealand Deer Velvet Antler On Muscle Strength & Endurance In Healthy Male University Athletes*, University of Otago and AgResearch Invermay, 1998

12. Media Release, New Zealand Game Industry Board, 18 February, 1998

13. NZ Game Industry Board

14. *The Deer Farmer*, July, 1998

14a. *Vitality*, Issue 3, Autumn 2000, Newsletter of the NZ Game Industry Board

15. *The Dominion*, Wellington, 19 February, 1998

15a. Suttie, Dr James M, and Stokes, *NZGIB Draft Technical Manual*, NZ Game Industry Board

16. Duarte, op. cit.

17. ibid. p.17

18. Archer and Palfreyman, op. cit.

19. "Hormone Receptors in Antlers: Research may be useful for Human Bone Disease," by Dr Graham Barrell (coauthor of Lynley Lewis' prize-winning paper

"Localisation of oestradiol receptors in antler tissue"), *The Deer Farmer*, December/January, 1991

20. Gerrard et al., op. cit.

21. Archer and Palfreyman, op. cit. p.41

22. Holmes, Peter, *Jade Remedies: A Chinese Herbal Reference for the West*, Snow Lotus Press, Boulder (1997)

23. *Daily News*, New Plymouth, 27 November, 1997

23a. Batchelder, Helen J., *Velvet Antler: A Literature Review*, North American Elk Breeders Association.

23b. Marshall, Lisa, Velvet Antler Under the Microscope, *Nutrition Science News*, March 2000. Reference to Albov, N.A., Information on the use of pantocrine in menopausal conditions, Altai Scientific Research Institute of Agriculture, 1969; Pantocrine Part 2:73-85.

24. Fulder, op. cit, p.195

25. Oriental Healing Arts Institute, Long Beach, California

26. Holmes, op. cit.

26a. Gold Mountain Trading Company Ltd., www.gold-mountain.co.nz

27. Archer and Palfreyman, op. cit. p.63

28. Suttie, Dr James M and Haines, Stephen R., *Evaluation of New Zealand Velvet Antler Efficacy and Diagnostic Testing*, AgResearch, Invermay Agricultural Centre, Mosgiel

29. Fulder, op. cit. p.215

30. ibid. p.218

31. ibid. p.217

32. ibid. p.218

32a. Archer and Palfreyman, op. cit.

33. ibid. p.222

34. Archer and Palfreyman, op. cit. p.57

35. Fulder op. cit. p.230

35a. Jamieson, James and Dorman, Dr. L.E., *Growth Hormone:Reversing Human Aging Naturally*, Safe Goods and Longevity News Network, East Canaan, CT, 1997

36. Archer and Palfreyman, op. cit.

37. Suttie, Dr James M, and Stokes, *NZGIB Draft Technical Manual*, NZ Game Industry Board.

38. NZGIB Media Release

39. Archer & Palfreyman, op. cit. p.58

40. ibid. p.72

41. Marshall, Lisa Anne, "Velvet Antler Under the Microscope," *Nutrition Science News*, March 2000, Vol.5, No. 3.

6

Testimonials

While science probes ever deeper into the secrets of velvet antler seeking the bioactive components that yield its unique potency, a growing number of Westerners are hearing about this ancient remedy and trying it for themselves.

Some, like Shelley Thomsen, who suffered from the painful symptoms of multiple sclerosis, have had their health and their lives dramatically changed after trying velvet antler. Shelley and her husband Clint, a deer farming couple from Hawkes Bay, New Zealand, learned the process of drying and crushing velvet in their kitchen at home, and began their own company, Gevir Products.

Shelley says, "I began taking my deer velvet and vitamin B when I was first diagnosed (with MS)... The next four years were attack free, something my neurologist found unusual. But over the next 4 years I gave up the velvet, vitamin B and rest and increased my workload again. I slowly had more and more attacks, of increasing severity each time, till my final one in 1990."

Now, after taking velvet daily she has not had a single attack and leads a very busy life with her business and two teenage children as well as playing squash, aerobics and jogging. She says, "1997-98 has been very good for me. I have no major reoccurring symptoms of my M.S. Just a few hot spots on my leg when getting too tired, which soon goes with rest."

Shelley believes the velvet, along with daily vitamin B complex, are the most beneficial supplements for her condition—as well as a healthy diet and time off to rest each day, if possible. As she says of the velvet, "It's not a cure by any means, but by taking it regularly I've certainly reduced the aches and pains and I've got heaps more energy." She continues, "Added bonuses of taking deer velvet are the loss of PMT and period pains. Most women would agree they are worth losing!"

Many other people, from a wide variety of ages and walks of life, have experienced the impressive therapeutic qualities of velvet antler, as the following letters testify:

...Since I started to use your velvet products, my well being has improved. I have more energy, a clear mind and better overall health. I have been using the products for just about 2 years now and wish to continue using them in the future. I have avoided the many flus people had contracted during the winter and I would say this is due to using velvet. I also find less fatigue than before I started the velvet. *S.F., Auckland*

...Taking velvet in autumn stops me getting winter colds. My shoulders are no longer sore, sprained ankle seems strong now, back pain gone and elbow OK too now. Could be just time cures? *M.D., Hawkes Bay*

...Since I have been taking deer velvet I very rarely suffer from the pain of arthritis in my knees and back, as I have told my doctor. Before I took the velvet I had very painful knees, sometimes I was in constant pain, which stopped me doing many of the things I enjoyed. Now I can't stay out of the garden. *C.D, Waipukurau, 79 years*

...Within three days of beginning a daily [velvet] dosage, the severe shoulder pain that I had been feeling for the past month had all but disappeared. This is pain that had defied treatment and which was made bearable only by consuming at least 2500mg of ibuprofen every day. Any other benefit from now on will be a bonus. *M.S., Seattle, Washington*

...I've just finished the second jar of Deer Velvet. I'm 74 years have arthritis in both knees bad... my knees aren't painful any more and I put this down to your product. I'm even back to a little dancing, I can't believe it. *N Powell*

...I have had rheumatoid arthritis for 5 years. The progressive problem was swollen and painful joints— especially hands, wrists, fingers, knees, ankles, shoulders and neck ....I now have no pain (was taking up to 20 painkillers a day) have got knuckles and ankles again, increased mobility everywhere and I am off my medication ...Thank you for a miracle. *J Redfern, Linton*

...I suffer from acute rheumatoid arthritis. Since taking the deer velvet I have noticed a significant improvement in my health. My energy level is high and I now suffer very little morning stiffness. *J Edmonds, Dannevirke*

...I started taking 2 capsules per day of your Deer

Velvet nearly a month ago and was suffering from arthritic joint pain in both hips, knee and shoulders and also muscular aches. After about 10 days there was a noticeable change for the better and now almost all pain has gone and I feel more vital. *S. D. Nelson*

...Another box of capsules please! Dad has given some to an old friend who was dying to paint his house in spite of the fact his shoulders were so stiff he couldn't raise his arms above shoulder height. After about 10 days he's all excited and reckons he's back to what he used to be many years ago! So the house is getting painted after all. Game old fella's eh! 70's and 80's and still painting houses. *C.E. Ruffell, Awanui*

...I just can't thank you enough. I received the antler on a day when I suffered a major asthma attack and should have ended up in hospital. But 20 minutes after taking 2 capsules, the wheezing reduced dramatically. *K.K., California*

...I am a mild asthmatic and haven't had an attack since using velvet, and haven't had any other medication. I feel more confident, and suffer less stress, which in my case can trigger an asthma attack. *J Coburn*

...I have found it most beneficial for PMT, menstruation pains and aching varicose veins. The headaches, aching veins and general 'dragging' feeling that are common during menstruation are no longer there. Now menstruation comes and goes without hardly being noticed. *D.P.*

... in my eighth month of pregnancy. I had a very low blood count which was causing extreme fatigue and low resistance to disease. The velvet has helped boost my blood count, strengthened my resistance and I am no longer constipated ... I plan to continue using the velvet throughout my pregnancy and breast-feeding as I find the general feeling of well being I have while taking it very important during this time. *V.W*

...I'm back on Velvet Antler. I was off for four months. I had bad hip joint problems, carpal tunnel and terrible hot flashes. I feel better all over. The hot flashes have lessened considerably. Before I got back to Velvet Antler my blood pressure had gone up. Two weeks later, with Velvet Antler, it had gone back to normal. I'm telling everyone. *Marie B.*

...I have suffered from Psoriasis for over 40 years, particularly on my scalp and various other parts of my body. After taking Deer Velvet capsules for only 3 weeks I have found my scalp has cleared completely and there is a marked improvement on the rest of my skin. I am delighted with the results. *C.M., Napier*

...Thank you again for the supply of Deer Velvet. As the proud owners of a Boxer dog this powder has definitely improved his quality of life. Angus (the Boxer) has for some time suffered from a severe skin condition affecting the lower levels of skin. After years of antibiotics and other medication—none of which seemed to work, we were told the only other option was to operate on the affected areas. Three years ago... I decided to try Deer Velvet powder on my dog. After only six weeks Angus was off all other medication, the legs were clear of all infection and he seemed happier all round... Angus is now eleven years old and still keeps up with us on our weekend treks. *C.E., Auckland*

...This stuff is amazing! I've been on it for three weeks and have felt a tremendous difference in the way I feel! Wow! Great stuff. Thank you for supplying this miracle "medicine"! *M.L., Santa Barbara, California*

...I'm 45 running a business, a toddler and teenager. Since I began taking velvet my energy has increased significantly. Now it's a necessary part of my diet & my only supplement. No winter colds or illness and my hair and fingernails are growing faster and stronger. *A.B., Auckland*

...At age 52, I feel a definite enhancement and strength with the use of pure deer velvet. I continue to be a high altitude mountaineer and maintain a strong sexual vitality. I can highly recommend this supplement. *S.J., Laytonville, California*

...I began taking Deer Velvet while I was a kidney dialysis patient. I added it to my vitamin and mineral regimen with the hope that it would help increase my energy level to overcome some of the ups and downs of my treatment. What actually happened was more than I expected. In combination with moderate exercise on the Nordic Track, I experienced noticeable muscle growth on my arms and shoulders. The additional strength and energy helped me to remain active in athletics in spite of my medical condition. I took one 300mg capsule a day for about a month, then I increased to two capsules a day. It was approximately three to four weeks after I had gone to two capsules a day before the effects started to be noticeable. *C.B., Chicago, Illinois*

...I love the velvet extract, gives me more endurance during workouts. *G.U., Oregon*

Megaceros giganteus,
the enormous extinct ancestor of today's deer.
From Deer of the World by G. Kenneth Whitehead

Appendix I

The Extraordinary Growth of Antlers

Antlers worthy to be termed 'royal' should have good length, widespread thick beams, long points, even balance, and handsome symmetry—in short, it should be a superb head.[1]

The *Song of Amergin*, which is perhaps the most famous poem from the Druidic bards of ancient Briton begins with the lines:

I am a stag of seven tines...
I am a hawk above the cliff...

The 'stag of seven tines' refers to seven points on each antler, giving fourteen in all which makes it worthy of the title 'imperial'— a 'royal' antler so-called, has twelve points. Describing the development of such a massive head of antlers, author Philip Holden writes:

In the succeeding years the whole antler of the 'stag' is not only larger, but the 'sur-royals' increase, breaking out into a series of snags forming like a cup, until is reached the full adult, a 'royal hart', with antlers three feet long, weighing as much as seventy pounds, and possessing from a dozen to forty points.[2]

The growth of a mature stag's magnificent head of antlers is truly unique. Unlike the horns of cattle, for example, which grow throughout the life of the animal, deer antlers are grown anew every year and are then cast, for the cycle of nature to repeat itself the following year.

Antler growth begins in the spring, sometime between August and October in the southern hemisphere, and between February and April in the north, immediately after the previous antlers are shed. Beginning as velvet antler budding from points on top of the skull called pedicles, they grow upwards with remarkable swiftness. After a month indications of the first branching tines, called bes or 'bez' tines, appear. By two months the next set of tines, the trey or 'trez' tines, are formed and by sixteen weeks the antlers have grown into their full size. As the new antlers grow they are comprised of cartilage, thick and rounded in appearance and warm and spongy to the touch. This cartilage is covered with a soft velvety fur.

As the antlers grow towards their full size they begin to harden and the cartilage transforms into bone. This begins from the base upwards as large quantities of calcium salts are deposited, until the antlers are fully calcified. Blood flow through the antlers remains high to the end of the velvet growth.

At this stage the velvet peels off, helped along by the stag who rubs or 'frays' his antlers against tree trunks or branches. The newly-frayed antlers are hard naked bone, quite unlike cattle horns that consist of a horny sheath covering a bone core. But soon the fresh cream coloured antlers become stained their characteristic dark brown tipped with light points.

Stags become fertile seasonally from the time their antlers reach full growth, around the month of February in the southern

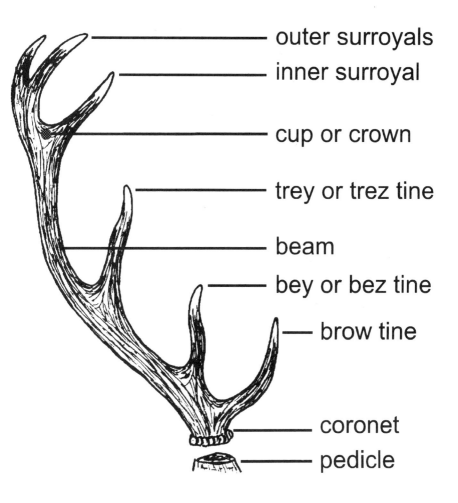

outer surroyals

inner surroyal

cup or crown

trey or trez tine

beam

bey or bez tine

brow tine

coronet

pedicle

Parts of the antler. *After Lentle & Saxon.*

hemisphere, and they remain fertile for up to eight months. Throughout the summer months stags feed on the lush vegetation and accumulate fat rapidly, preparing themselves for the arduous rutting season ahead when there is no time to eat or rest and they remain lean for the rest of the year. Coming up to the rut the stag develops a mane of thick hair, his neck swells and he likes to roll around in wallows of muddy water. He also develops a 'lion-like roar' or a 'bull-like bellow' that reverberates across the mountain valleys and can be heard for more than a mile away. It is in this state of intense potency he challenges his rivals, or prepares to meet the challenge.

The size of the antlers depends greatly on the age of the stag and its state of health. While yearlings, often referred to as 'spikers' only grow a pair of single spikes, two year olds generally have four to eight points while fully grown stags have ten to twelve points or more. The actual shape of the antler, its curvature and thickness, is largely dependent on its genetic heritage and it has been noted that over time deer in the various herds around New Zealand have displayed certain distinctive features in their antler form, like a family signature, which have been recognised from their ancestral bloodlines in England.

The shape of antlers also differs considerably among the various species of deer, ranging from the finer more delicate tines of the White-tailed deer and Sika, to the heavy palmated antlers of the Fallow buck, a species that was also liberated into New Zealand during the late 1800s.

Strange aberrations also occur from time to time, such as an 'ugly monstrosity' recorded by the hunter and author Donne, a freak stag's head shot in 1696 bearing no less than sixty-two points.[3] Magnificent stags with as many as sixty-six points have also been reported in Central Europe, according to Holden ..."and quite doubling in weight the twenty to thirty stone of the finest Scottish stags."[4] But even the most magnificent head pales in comparison to the huge *Megaceros giganteus,* the enormous ancestor of today's deer that once grazed on neolithic plains.

The rapid growth of deer antler from its velvet stage to hard calcified bone has been the focus of intense scientific curiosity, and so too has the connection between the sexual life of the stag and the growth of his antlers. As the blood flows through the young velvet it is rich with nutrients, hormones and other growth enhancing substances. When the blood flow ceases, when the antlers are at their fullest development and the blood is diverted into the other body organs, the stag is at his greatest

Fallow bucks in antler.
Photo courtesy Harry Bimler

sexual potency and vitality, ready for the roar and the rutting season.

Authors Roger Lentle and Frank Saxon observed that, "If a female fawn is given injections of the male hormone testosterone, she will develop pedicles and subsequent antler; if a male fawn is castrated at birth, thus stopping testosterone production, he will not develop pedicles."[5]

Here lies a hint as to why deer velvet has gained such a wide reputation as an aphrodisiac, and why the mighty stag with his thick mane of hair, powerful body and great rack of antlers evokes the primal instinct in man.

THE VELVETING CODE OF PRACTICE

Whenever the subject of deer velvet arises there is often concern raised about the treatment of the deer. The idea of breeding stags for their antlers is a new and uncertain subject, at least in the Western world. In Asian countries such as China velvet antler has been harvested for hundreds, if not thousands, of years and deer farming is regarded as a traditional way of life. In New Zealand the highest standards have been set for the welfare of the animals, not just on the velveting issue, but on their overall care and management.

To ensure the humane treatment of deer veterinarians have been appointed to supervise the velveting, with support from the Animal Welfare Advisory Committee. Under an agreed Code of Practise farmers undergo a training program where they are assessed as being competent to velvet their own stags under the supervision of a vet. Veterinarians are legally responsible for the use of prescription drugs to provide adequate analgesia and may only prescribe them to deer farmers who have passed the necessary certification.

The velveting itself is a quick procedure and the stags are immediately released to graze, in fact it is one of the few human interventions in their otherwise comfortable life. In the wild a mature stag has a very short life expectancy, living with the ever-present threat of the hunter in all but the most remote regions, and driven by a constant search for food. On the farm deer are valuable animals and are treated with care, kept healthy and well fed through even the lean winter months.

Quite apart from the value of the harvested velvet, from the earliest days of deer farming it was the practice of farmers to remove the stags' growing antlers because as dangerous as they are in the wild, even the young spikes are a lethal weapon in a herd of young stags. The timing of velvet harvesting is crucial to the high quality of the velvet and most top grade velvet is harvested within 50-55 days after casting last season's antlers. If the velvet is left too long it becomes over-calcified which reduces its medicinal properties.

NOTES

1. Donne, T.E., *Red Deer Stalking in New Zealand*, The Halcyon Press, Auckland, (1986)
2. Holden, Philip, *New Zealand Hunters' Paradise*, p22, Hodder and Stoughton, Auckland (1985)
3. Donne, op. cit. p.197
4. Holden, op. cit. p.2
5. Lentle, Roger and Saxton, Frank, *Red Deer in New Zealand: A complete hunting manual*, p.166, David Bateman Ltd, "Golden Heights," Auckland (1991)

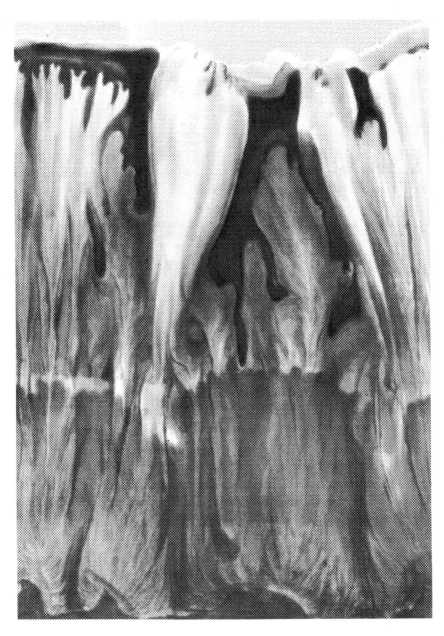

Crystallisation of 1% Silver Nitrate
solution followed by Stag's Urine

Appendix II

ANTLER FORCES IN NATURE

As mentioned previously, traditional Oriental medicine has always perceived a strong affinity existing between deer velvet antler and the kidneys in the human organism. This connection brought to mind something I had come across years ago while studying the work of a German research scientist named Lily Kolisko. Among her published works is a book called *Agriculture of Tomorrow*, written with her husband Eugen; a fascinating in-depth study of the bio-dynamic method of farming and gardening. Central to this method is the use of certain preparations, both animal and herbal, which are used in minute amounts in the compost or on the land itself, to promote healthy plant growth. The principle could be related to homeopathy, which is a form of medicine using highly diluted substances to treat the symptoms of disease.

Among these preparations, there is one in particular which uses the bladder from a freshly killed stag. The bladder is stuffed with yarrow flowers (yarrow is considered to be a herbal remedy for kidney and bladder problems) and hung in the sun over the summer months. During autumn and winter, the bladder with its herbal stuffing is buried in the earth until the following spring when it is dug up and added in very small amounts to the manure or compost heap. Research has discovered that this preparation has a more potent effect on plant growth than any artificial fertiliser. While this may seem unusual to anyone unfamiliar with this system of organic farming, it has proved highly successful to innumerable bio-dynamic farmers around the world.

Further studies by the Koliskos on animal health focussed on a process called capillary dynamolysis. This involved the crystallisation of animal urine combined with metallic salts in solution on filter paper. The pictures formed in this way are said to demonstrate the life-force (or ch'i) of the animal, given form by the presence of the metallic salts. Quite distinctive pictures formed on the filter paper as the urine crystalised, depending on the metals being used. When stag's urine was used combined with silver nitrate, the pictures took on a rather extraordinary form. Time and time again, in similar experiments performed with many stags, the urine formed very characteristic and distinctive antler-like formations.

The Koliskos describe these crystallisation pictures as revealing the connection that exists between the antlers and the urine: the same force that forms the antlers "streams through the kidney system, penetrates the urine" and is a unique quality of the stag. The crystallisation pictures formed by the urine of the cow, horse, or pig, are quite different, and so too were the pictures formed by the urine of a stag with a diseased bladder where the antler-like forms were completely absent.

Perhaps in this bio-dynamic approach to farming the Koliskos have provided us with a way of looking at the animal-plant-earth connection in terms of energy as well as chemistry and matter. In this respect their research has an affinity with Oriental philosophy and medicine with its emphasis on a wholistic view of the relationship between human, earth and cosmos.

Kolisko, E & L, Agriculture of Tomorrow, *Kolisko Archive Publications, Bournemouth, England. (1978)*

FURTHER READING

Banwell, D. Bruce, *The Royal Stags of Windsor*, The Halcyon Press, Auckland, 1994

Bennett, Bob, *Traditional Trade in Velvet*, Proceedings World Deer Congress, 1993

Bimler, Harry, *My Deer Life*, The Halcyon Press, Auckland, 1995

Caughley, Graeme, *The Deer Wars: The Story of Deer in New Zealand*, Heinemann Publishers, Auckland, 1983

Dean, Ward, M.D., and Morgenthaler, John, *Smart Drugs & Nutrients*, Vol. 1, Smart Publications, Petaluma, California (1990)

Deer Antler Velvet—*An ancient Oriental medicine enjoys growing popularity in the West*—published by The Deer Farmer/Game Industry Board 1992

DeerVelvet.org — Deer Antler Velvet public awareness website www.deervelvet.org

Donne, T.E., *Red Deer Stalking in New Zealand*, The Halcyon Press, Auckland, 1986, first published by Constable and Company Ltd, London, 1924

Fennessy, P.F., *Velvet Antler: The Product and Pharmacology*, AgResearch Invermay, New Zealand

Fennessy, Dr Peter, and Duncan, Syd., "NZ Red velvet antler compares well," *The Deer Farmer*, August, 1992

Holden, Philip, *The Golden Years of Hunting in New Zealand*, Hodder and Stoughton, Auckland, 1983

—*New Zealand: Hunters' Paradise*, Hodder & Stoughton, Auckland, 1985

Kamen, Betty and Paul, *The Remarkable Healing Power of Velvet Antler*, Nutrition Encounter, Novato, California 1999

King, Carolyn M, ed., *The Handbook of New Zealand Mammals*, Auckland Oxford University Press in association with The Mammal Society, NZ Branch. C.N. Challies, author, 1990

Suttie, Dr James M, and Stokes, *NZGIB Draft Technical Manual*, New Zealand Game Industry Board.

Teeguarden, Ron, *Chinese Herbal Tonics*, Cha Yuan Press, California, 1991

Walton, Trevor, "Korea: The GIB's big success story," *The Deer Farmer*, November, 1991

—"Bridging the agri-cultural barriers," *The Deer Farmer*, Sept. 1992

—"Assured future for quality velvet," *The Deer Farmer*, June, 1994

Whitehead, G.K., *Deer of the World*, Constable & Co., London, 1972

RESOURCE DIRECTORY

- Producers of 100% deer velvet capsules and bulk powder: Gevir Products N.Z. Ltd, 189 Nelson Road, Takapau, Hawkes Bay, New Zealand. Ph/Fax: +64-6-855-8404. www.gevir.co.nz email: gevir@xtra.co.nz

- Pure New Zealand deer velvet antler and velvet antler extracts, including herbal formulas, available from Gold Mountain Trading Company Ltd, PO Box 267, Katikati, New Zealand. Ph: +64-7-549-3492 Fax: +64-7-549-3496. www.velvex.com email: velvet@velvex.com

- Quality New Zealand dietary supplements including Titan Extra, standardised 33:1 deer velvet extract, and Qu-Up, a velvet extract energy tonic with herbs and vitamins. Contact Happy Families, PO Box 336, Drury, South Auckland, New Zealand. Ph: +64-9-294-8444 Fax: +64-9-294-7783. www.honeybalm.com email: timandjenny@honeybalm.com